The Talking Revolution

How Creative Conversation Can Change the World

Peter Osborn
and
Eddy Canfor-Dumas

PORT MEADOW PRESS

About the Authors

Peter Osborn teaches the skills of conversation to people of all ages, in schools, businesses, local authorities, charities and social enterprises. He has written and presented a wide range of videos, produced books and comics for children, and delivered workshops and professional development programmes for a variety of organisations, including British Telecom, the Communication Trust, the Stephen Lawrence Trust and Essex County Council. He is also a visiting lecturer at the University of London and a trustee of the bereavement charity The Loss Foundation.

Eddy Canfor-Dumas is a writer and an adviser in conflict management. He has written best-selling books and award-winning TV dramas; supported the development of conflict prevention policy in Parliament; worked with the Commonwealth Secretariat, OSCE, NATO and the Swedish Armed Forces; been a visiting lecturer at the UK Defence Academy and a member of the Chief of Defence Staff's Strategy Forum; and co-led the international civil-military initiative 'Understand to Prevent', which produced practical guidance on the military contribution to the prevention of violent conflict. Eddy is also a Samaritans listening volunteer.

Acknowledgements

The ideas put forward in these pages are founded on the thoughts and work of many others. We're especially indebted to Professor Gerard Egan, Andrew Bailey, Adrian Hosford, Daisaku Ikeda and Marshall Rosenberg, all of whom have significantly helped shape our thinking over many years.

We're also hugely grateful to family, friends and colleagues who took the time and trouble to read the text in its various drafts and offer many helpful criticisms and suggestions. Along with Gerry, Andrew and Adrian, our thanks go to Rose Bellingham, Jo Broadwood, Mitsu Carvalho, Mandy Cuttica, Hilary Dodman, Mirco Frassin, Jane Franks, Ben Freedman, Marie-Victoire Garcia, Max Glaskin, Sally Glaskin, David Hare, John Hindes, Brenda James, Jason Jarrett, Roy Leighton, Simon Linnell, Mike Martin, Wendy Martin, Rob Moore, Tony Morris, Jenny Rogers, Roz Scott, Angela Southon – and, of course, to Annie and Coralyn, Alexander and Tom, and Lily and Emily. Together, your input has made this book so much richer and stronger.

Finally, it's no exaggeration to say that we've been shaped and influenced by everything we've read and every conversation we've ever had on this vast and vastly important topic of how we talk and listen to each other. We're part of a much wider community that has been working at how to establish and improve communication between human beings for many years, usually out of sight and unrecognised. And that includes all those who have taken part in our workshops – we suspect we've learnt at least as much from you as we hope you might have gleaned from us.

So to **everyone** who has helped inspire and shape this book – thank you. The conversation continues…

Port Meadow Press
43 Leckford Road, Oxford OX2 6HY
Registered Co. No. 4405635

ISBN 978-1-9998379-0-7

PORT MEADOW PRESS

Contents

Introduction

We've got a big problem, we human beings. Bigger than plastic in the oceans and toxins in the air, bigger even than climate change. It's how we talk and listen to each other.

It's the basis for **everything** we do – and will need to do – together. Yet so much of our communication washes around in a sea of confusion, conflict and dysfunction – at home, at work, in society and in the world.

'That's life,' some will say. 'It's normal.' But it needn't be. We can do better. We *have* to do better. Because if we don't improve things soon we could all be scuppered, as the challenges we face threaten to overwhelm us.

That's why we need a revolution – a **talking revolution**. We need a massive, worldwide improvement in how we communicate. How we talk to each other. How we listen to each other. How we understand and are understood by each other. We've had a revolution in the technology that connects us around the world, in the hardware and the software – now we need a revolution in the 'humanware', the *quality* of how we actually communicate with each other, one to one.

We need this talking revolution to happen everywhere – at the kitchen table and the conference table, in the boardroom and the bedroom, the classroom and the office; in the international community and the community centre; in the pub, in the street, on the bus, online, offline. Everywhere.

We also need it to involve everyone – young, old, male, female, rich, poor, straight, gay, able-bodied, disabled, black, white and every other shade too. Because *everyone* has the

1

potential to become a talking revolutionary and to benefit from better, stronger connections with other people.

And we need this talking revolution *urgently*. All around the world people are realising that we have to collaborate on an ever-increasing scale, at every level, if we're to find common solutions to the challenges that face us nationally, regionally and globally. To do that we urgently need a step-change in the quality of how we talk to and understand each other one-to-one. Just imagine the benefits that could flow at all levels – internationally, locally and domestically. Not just in the emotional pain that can be avoided by developing greater understanding and empathy between each other – huge though that would be in itself – but in the gains that could be generated *in all areas of life*. Imagine a world in which miscommunication and misunderstanding are minimised, and mutual understanding maximised.

A pipe-dream?

No – because most, if not all, misunderstanding is actually avoidable. And because *you* can become a talking revolutionary *right now*, in your very next conversation with the very next person you talk to. You are at the centre of your own, unique world, so when *you* decide to change, when you decide to engage with the people of your world differently, your world *has* to change in response – whatever the communication challenges you face.

And as you change your world for the better, so others in your world will be inspired to follow suit and the talking revolution will unfold around you, step-by step. The power is in your hands, our hands, all of us, singly and collectively.

Talking revolutionaries are ordinary people who consciously take it upon themselves to bring about a revolution in talking and listening in their own, unique environment – family, friends, colleagues, neighbours, whatever – through developing the art of **creative conversation**. This is a distillation into seven essential elements of what we all do when we're communicating at our best. It's absolutely free, totally doable, extraordinarily effective and easily learned – by anyone, by *you* – so that individually and together we can transform the **three pains** that plague us all.

THE THREE PAINS

First, there's the **personal** pain of being unable to talk meaningfully with someone who's significant to you – a family member, a partner, a colleague, a friend.

Who hasn't replayed a painful conversation in their head and agonised about how it went so badly off-track, or what they might have said to bring about a better outcome? Who hasn't felt the frustration of being unable to break through a seemingly impenetrable barrier with a particular person to reach (again) a point of mutual understanding and connection? And how many relationships – families – have broken down because that barrier couldn't be breached? In the UK, at least, it's an alarming number. A 2017 report[1] highlights that almost 50% of all children in the UK are no longer living with both their parents by the time they sit their mid-teen exams; while for children in the poorest communities, nearly half have already seen their parents split up by the time they start school at five years old. And as the report notes:

> When we talk about family breakdown we don't simply mean separation or divorce; both family structure and relationship quality are increasingly understood to have an important impact on outcomes for children. We shouldn't ignore either.

But the personal pain of miscommunication doesn't come just from relationships that break down; increasingly it's the result of feeling unable to connect with anyone at all. Another 2017 study[2] concluded that the 'developed' world is experiencing a growing 'loneliness epidemic' that could be as damaging to individuals and society as obesity or smoking. In the UK not only are more and more people living alone, but some nine million of them say that they feel often or always lonely.[3] So serious is the problem that in January 2018 the UK government appointed the world's first ever Minister for Loneliness, charged with delivering a strategy to address isolation nationwide, across all age ranges.

A talking revolution aimed at transforming any of these personal pains would reap enormous benefits. If you become a talking revolutionary that might well be precisely where you decide to target your efforts – even on just one particular person – and that's fine.

On the other hand, you might decide to focus on transforming the **group pain** of belonging to (or being responsible for) a team or organisation that's suffering from poor interpersonal communication. For some reason – or several – the members of the group don't seem able to talk to each other in a way that generates a healthy, productive atmosphere. Perhaps senior figures in the group are at loggerheads and the negative ripples are affecting everyone else. Or the culture somehow encourages a 'silo mentality', or groupthink and conformity, and discourages challenge and creativity, even if no one in the group consciously means it to. Or maybe internal competition or lack of trust between individuals or subgroups means that information is deliberately withheld from rivals and so damages the group as a whole.

Individuals tend to think they have a limited ability to affect group behaviour, especially if the group is large and/or they don't have senior status – but that's not necessarily the case. In many groups an individual is able to affect others not through their status or expertise but through what's called their 'referent influence' – their character, values or other personal qualities. In effect, their influence is 'given' to them by others in the group because for some reason they like, admire, trust, respect or believe in that person. Which means that a talking revolutionary, by practising creative conversation, will always be able to maximise their referent influence in a group, whatever their status; while two or more talking revolutionaries can positively turbo-charge it. Given that examples of group dysfunction arising from poor communication are so commonplace, the transformative potential of a talking revolution within teams and organisations of all kinds is enormous. (More of this in Chapter 2.)

In some ways, the third of the three pains is the greatest challenge of all. This is **societal pain**, experienced by those living in conflicted and polarising societies. The pain has always been present, of course, to different degrees in different societies, but today it has a powerful accelerant – the internet. The result is that a number of societies that until recently appeared stable seem to be steadily splintering into cultural and political 'tribes', who find it increasingly difficult to break out of their own echo-chambers, let alone build bridges to other camps. As Peter Senge[4] acutely observed at the end of the last century, 'In a sense we are running an historic social experiment today. We are experimenting with whether or not a society can hold itself together without the core process that has always bound societies, the process of conversation.'[5]

Take the story of Pepin County, Wisconsin. A farming area of some 7,000 people, it hadn't voted for a Republican president for more than forty years. But in 2016 it went solidly for Donald Trump, much to the shock of the local Democrats. What the vote laid bare was a cleft that had been deepening in the county for years, not just between Democrats and Republicans, liberals and conservatives, but between urbanite incomers and rural families who'd lived there for generations. And since the vote things definitely haven't improved. As the journalist Michael Kruse reports:[6]

Republicans and Democrats, Trump voters and Trump

haters, natives and newcomers, told me the same thing: The gap between them has widened. And this colder, more rigid strain of political division, I heard repeatedly, has curdled a regional habit of happy-faced avoidance into something that feels more like a toxic silence...

People here, in this demographically homogeneous, almost entirely white community, have plenty to say about all this – they just have chosen not to say it to each other. If there is a wall that Trump has built, it's not the 'big, beautiful' one on the Mexican border – it's the figurative wall that has risen in places like Pepin County, Wisconsin.

This is a form of societal pain, a pain that's manifested collectively but felt personally, by individuals such as Andrea Myklebust. She moved from the big city to her smallholding in Pepin County in 2005, to weave and sculpt and live off her chickens and sheep. Everything was pretty idyllic – until the 2016 vote. As a Democrat, Myklebust was devastated. Suddenly, she felt herself to be surrounded by people she barely knew, aliens almost, and hostile ones at that.

But she also found herself facing a major dilemma. Mitch Nelson, the farmer who supplied the winter hay for her sheep, was a Trump voter (she assumed) and buying from him again this winter just felt...wrong. But eventually she overcame her reluctance and sent him a text message – could he sell her thirty bales? Nelson replied quickly, but in the negative – a poor harvest meant he could only sell her two and no, he didn't know where she might find more. Fair enough, one might think – but for Myklebust, it was the final straw.

For Myklebust, the hay wasn't just hay – it was her last tangible connection to a Trump voter. And she read Nelson's curt last text as a door slammed shut, proof that these sorts of interactions with people she saw as less than like-minded were pointless. If she had spoken to Nelson, picked up the phone or even just asked him to deliver those two remaining bales, she might have learned something that could have corrected her assumption, or at the very least preserved an admittedly tenuous bond with a neighbor. But she didn't. Despite what she had vowed to me a year ago,[7] she hasn't engaged. She has done the opposite. She has retreated. She's ending her involvement with the board of the local history museum, and she left her position atop an area merchants association – not because these are groups stocked with Republicans, but due to her persistently grim mood. A couple of months ago, she said, she unfriended 'the last conservative' in her Facebook feed.

Everything she considers so objectionable that is happening because of Trump, she believes, is happening because of these people in this place. 'I cannot separate what I am seeing modeled and demonstrated and articulated, again and again and again, at the national level – I can't separate it from the people who voted for that around here,' Myklebust said. 'And that's what it comes down to. I just don't want to have a political conversation with anybody who thought that was OK a year ago, and thinks it's OK now.'

Kruse visited Mitch Nelson and discovered that he felt no animosity whatsoever towards his Democrat neighbour. In fact, he didn't know or care how she'd voted. He simply didn't have the hay. But even learning this didn't change Myklebust's attitude. The die had been cast, the Rubicon crossed and there was no turning back.

She's not alone. Her reaction has been replicated throughout the county, on both sides of the divide. And the one (failed) public attempt at dialogue has only hardened the feeling that trying to talk across that divide is a waste of time.

The story of Pepin County is, in microcosm, the current story of the USA. And Brexit Britain. And Scottish/Catalan/Basque independence. And rising populist/nationalist movements throughout Europe. And, in differing hues, the story of apparently irreconcilable political and cultural differences around the world. It's the story of a 'cold war' polarisation that could last for years, decades even; or that could, with the right combination of causes and conditions, turn 'hot' and lead to the violence that so often characterises deeply divided societies. Perhaps, above all, it's here that we need a talking revolution – and the talking revolutionaries who will make it happen. How? By consciously seeking to (re)connect people and (re)build trust through the practice of creative conversation.

Which is what, exactly?

CREATIVE CONVERSATION

Distilled from our years of working in dialogue and conflict management – and drawing on the acute insights of many others working in these areas, past and present – creative conversation is an approach to talking that *actively seeks to create something of value in every conversation*. Specifically, creative conversation aims to meet the needs of everyone involved – including, of course, our own. And at its most basic level, creative conversation seeks to create, revive or deepen our connection with another human being.

Most of us have probably had some experience of creative conversation, though we probably haven't called it that. At its best, it's the type of verbal exchange that enriches and energises us, that clears our minds and even uplifts us. And just as tasty food can range from a bite-sized snack to a three-course meal, so creative conversation can range from a brief chat to a life-changing dialogue – it's the quality that counts. But for many of us talking like this is a hit-and-miss affair, and perhaps all the more significant because truly creative conversation can be an infrequent, even rare, event.

It needn't be, though.

In this book, we explain how you can consistently make the seven essential elements of creative conversation the cornerstone of your daily life. These are:

- the Three Principles of Personal Responsibility, Openness and Creativity
- the Three Practices of Understanding, Challenging and Being Understood
- the art of Conversation Management

Through practising one or more (ideally all) of these elements, you can maximise your ability to transform any of the three pains - personal, group, societal - into tangible benefit and start an everyday talking revolution to change your world for the better. One conversation at a time.

So this book is not just about how to have difficult conversations or using dialogue to deal with conflicts - although it can be employed successfully in both those contexts. It's about making a **fundamental** shift - a revolution - in how we interact verbally with each other, a shift that's rooted in the everyday. It's about the small things as well as the big things, the domestic as well as the global. It's about how we can all talk and listen to each other in a way that strengthens the connection between us, even when we disagree.

FUNDAMENTAL NEEDS

Underpinning everything is a focus on fundamental human needs. These are the same in all cultures and in all historical periods — they're fundamental to what makes us human. But exactly how we meet them changes at different times and in different societies. They're also weighted differently in each individual; we all have the need for safety, for example, but for some people it's much more important than for others.

(See Appendix A for an exercise to help identify the fundamental human needs that are important to you , which also shape your values.)

The key point is that we're all driven by the (often unconscious) urge to satisfy the needs that are important to us. We adopt various, often ineffective, strategies to do this and experience positive emotions when our needs are met and negative emotions when they're not. So the essential elements of creative conversation are focused on meeting a range of fundamental human needs – for connection, respect, clarity, understanding, hope and many others. These are crucial to relationship-building, *regardless of who we're talking to or what we're talking about.*

Creative conversation, based on an awareness of fundamental human needs, is a manifestation of our humanity operating at its best to get to the heart of things. It's not about winning arguments or converting others to a particular point of view (although either of those things might happen). Rather, it's about seeking to identify what's *really* going on in the other person and in ourselves, and trying to create something of value for everyone involved. This point will emerge with increasing clarity in the course of this book, especially through the stories and case studies; all of which (unless explicitly stated otherwise) are closely based on things that have actually happened, even if we've changed details here and there to respect the privacy of those involved.

TO RECAP...

These, then, are the essential elements of the talking revolution:

1. Personal happiness and well-being, effective group collaboration and flourishing societies are all ultimately founded on healthy human relationships.

2. Healthy human relationships are founded on the way in which we talk and listen to each other.
3. One-to-one conversation that is responsible, open and creative is our most developed form of communication. It enables us to understand each other, to challenge each other in ways that are wise, respectful and productive, and to be understood by each other in return.
4. This process, which we call 'creative conversation', is focused on identifying and meeting the fundamental human needs which lie at the heart of our well-being.

If creative conversation is the cause, a talking revolution is the effect, which is felt in the difference that even one creative conversation can make. Transforming the personal pain of fractured relationships can lead to longer, happier life. Transforming the group pain of poor communication can lead to us working better together. And transforming the societal pain of polarised communities and perspectives can help us mend the world.

This book is a call to budding talking revolutionaries everywhere.

> **Efforts to reach out and engage others in dialogue**
> **with the aim of fostering mutual understanding**
> **and bringing people closer together may seem**
> **ordinary and unexciting, but they in fact**
> **constitute a bold and daring challenge to create**
> **a new era of human civilisation.'**
> *Daisaku Ikeda*[8]

Part One

Foundations

Part One consists of two chapters.

Chapter 1: We Are Relationships looks at how our individual well-being is based on the unique network of personal relationships we each have, and the vital role that communication plays in the quality of those relationships.

Chapter 2: Three Principles of Creative Conversation proposes three basic principles– Personal Responsibility, Openness and Creativity – as the foundation for the creative conversations that will positively transform our relationships.

Chapter 1

We Are Relationships

'If you want to have a long, happy and fulfilled life, how should you invest your time and effort right now?'

It's a brilliant question. It comes from Robert Waldinger, the fourth director of the Harvard Study of Adult Development, the world's longest continuous study into happiness and well-being. Back in 1938 his predecessors started collecting data on the health, work, income, relationships and general well-being of 268 young men in Boston, Massachusetts – all undergraduates at Harvard University. A few years later a separate study started collecting data at the other end of the social spectrum – 456 teenage boys from troubled families in the city's poorest neighbourhoods – and after a while the two studies merged. Every two years, for as long as they've been able to draw breath, all of the men have been interviewed, brain-scanned, blood-tested and had the minutiae of their personal and working lives recorded in detail.

'So what have we learned?' asks Waldinger.[1] 'What are the lessons that come from the tens of thousands of pages of information that we've generated on these lives? Well, the lessons aren't about wealth or fame or working harder and harder. The clearest message that we get from this 75-year study is this – good relationships keep us happier and healthier. Period.'

Good relationships keep us healthier and happier… Is that it? What about exercise, and diet – and money? They must make a difference too – surely?

Not really, according to Waldinger. Overwhelmingly, the 724 life stories recorded in the Harvard Study show that 'people who are more socially connected to family, to friends, to community are happier. They're physically healthier and they live longer than people who are less well connected. And the experience of loneliness turns out to be toxic. People who are more isolated than they want to be from others find that they are less happy, their health declines earlier in mid-life, their brain functioning declines sooner and they live shorter lives than people who are not lonely.' Nursing a grudge over many years against a family member can be especially toxic. On the other hand, early disadvantages – a deprived or unhappy childhood, say – can be overcome through at least one close, loving or supportive relationship. We don't have to be prisoners of our past.

The Harvard Study is not alone in its view of what really matters. A 2016 report into well-being produced by a team at the London School of Economics concluded that getting richer certainly doesn't translate into getting happier. According to the team's head, 'The evidence shows that the things that matter most for our happiness and for our misery are our social relationships and our mental and physical health.'[2]

Anecdotal evidence from around the world lends further weight to this thesis. For example, take the longevity of the inhabitants of the tiny Italian village of Acciaroli, south of Naples. More than ten per cent of its population of 700 are centenarians, compared to between 3-4 per cent for the region as a whole (and a mere 0.02 per cent in the USA), and researchers want to know why. They've looked at the locals' genes, their diet, how much they exercise and various environmental factors, and have concluded that all of these do indeed play a part. But they also noticed that sexual activity is 'rampant'.

To put it more delicately, Acciarolians put great store by their relationships. As a visiting journalist reported:[3]

> But it wasn't until we met Antonio and Amina that I really got an insight into what makes people in Acciaroli live so long. Antonio celebrated his 100th birthday last February …
>
> The secret of his longevity, he insisted, was 'this beautiful woman, the woman of my life.' Amina, 93, smiled shyly. Spry and good-humoured, she still writes poetry, and recites it easily from memory. Her favourite is a poem she dedicated to Antonio.
>
> > By the sea, the waves put my soul at rest
> > I saw a little boat approach, a fisherman laying nets
> > When he got closer, I looked at him and he smiled at me
> > He invited me on board for a ride, it was a pleasure trip
> > I saw seagulls flying around, fighting with the other fishermen
> > I was taken by the beauty of the sea, and I became the bride of the fisherman.
>
> As she spoke the final line, she reached out and caressed Antonio's chin. Love and affection – plus all that other healthy stuff, perhaps – are the real secret ingredients of their longevity.

In fact, it's not unusual for residents of Acciaroli in their 80s or 90s to take a new partner when their spouse dies, supporting another conclusion of the Harvard Study. 'The people in our 75-year study who were the happiest in retirement,' says Robert Waldinger, 'were the people who had actively worked to replace workmates with new playmates.'

Put simply, there is a rising tide of evidence emerging now from many different disciplines – psychology, neurology, education, even economics – all pointing in the same basic direction: if we want to live long, healthy, happy lives, we shouldn't look first at our bank balance, our possessions or our job titles – important though these might be. We should look at the strength and depth of our interactions with the people around us. Meaningful relationships aren't the icing on the cake of life – they're its main ingredients.

> **Life is relationships. The rest is details.**
> *Gary Smalley*[4]

So, here's a question. If meaningful relationships are indeed the key to a long, happy and fulfilling life, what *can* we do right now to create more value in our relationships? And not just with people to whom we're already close but in *all* of our relationships, so that we're surrounded by a human environment that is increasingly rich in support and meaning?

The answer is to improve how we communicate. And a great way to do this is to adopt the Three Principles and Three Practices of creative conversation. In a nutshell, creative conversation means 'listening in a way that helps people talk and talking in a way that helps people listen' in order to meet one or more of the basic human needs of all involved, especially the needs for connection and understanding. By holding more and more creative conversations we can improve our ability to communicate with others in all areas of life – family, work, friendships, even with supposedly remote and impersonal institutions. And through this improved communication not only can we become happier; the chances are we'll live longer, too. Research in many fields is showing that relationships, communication and our physical and mental development and well-being are inseparably and profoundly interconnected. For example, consider the orphans of Nicolae Ceaușescu's Romania.

Ceaușescu believed the Stalinist dogma that population

growth automatically leads to economic growth and, as Romania's Communist president, promoted fertility as state policy. Abortion was severely limited and contraception banned. The population duly expanded but the expected economic growth failed to materialise and families slipped deeper and deeper into poverty. More and more children were abandoned into state care – in reality they weren't orphans, simply 'separated from their parents' – but the state orphanages were themselves strapped for cash, under-staffed and shockingly unfit for purpose.

When the Ceaușescu regime was toppled in December 1989 the world was appalled at what was exposed. Stick-thin children tied to their beds. Physically and mentally damaged children who couldn't walk or talk. Children who rocked back and forth all day, hands flapping, soaked in their urine. Tales of staff cruelty and neglect, and of abuse and bullying between the children themselves, were legion.

The response was a frenzy of relief activity – truckloads of food, clothes and toys sent from the West – and coming the other way, damaged children, often adopted with minimal legal oversight. A less visible response was the interest of Western psychologists and behavioural scientists. Might something positive come from this huge, unplanned experiment in denying institutionalised children the stimulation of normal human relationships? What could be learnt?

Their studies showed that the effects on the children depended on several factors – how long they had been in the system, what age they were on entry and exit, and where exactly they'd been held, for example – and children who'd been placed at a very young age and for only six months or so emerged pretty much unscathed. In general, though, the children showed signs of impaired mental and emotional development. They had difficulty engaging with other people, with concentrating and learning, and with forming relationships. As adults, roughly four out of five still experience a much higher rate of social, emotional or cognitive problems than contemporaries who were brought up with normal human interaction.

More recent studies in child development[5] and advances in brain scanning support the conclusions of the research into the Romanian orphans. They imply that neglecting to stimulate a child – 'communication deprivation' – can actually hinder the crucial early stages of neurological development, while separating a child from his or her parents at an early age can cause trauma that has a range of long-term emotional and psychological harms. On the other hand, children who have improved language development (in the first three years in particular) will later show better intellectual development and educational achievement. Thinking develops through language and language develops through thinking.

Children with better language skills will also develop better social skills, which is important in helping them find a positive place in their peer group, especially as they get older. But children who struggle with verbal interaction tend to be isolated or rejected, or will find other ways of establishing themselves that might not be socially acceptable or productive; and research confirms that people in prison and young offenders' institutions do indeed have a high incidence of speech, language and communication difficulties. David Ramsbotham, Her Majesty's Chief Inspector of Prisons in the late 1990s, once said he became acutely aware of the link during a visit to young offenders' institution in Scotland. 'I was walking around with the governor when he suddenly said, "If I had to get rid of all my staff, the last one out of the gate would be my speech and language therapist."'[6]

But even outside prison or where there is no childhood neglect, so many lives fail to grow to their full potential simply because we don't use our inherent capacity for communication nearly as well as we might.

COMMUNICATION IS A
FUNDAMENTAL HUMAN NEED

In large part, this is because we don't fully appreciate that communication is at the core of how we function and develop, both as individuals and as social animals. It is, arguably, the most important human need after our physical needs for survival. One key aim of the talking revolution is to raise awareness of this and its crucial importance to all of us as individuals, as groups and as a species.

At the *individual* level – and as the Romania story and child development studies show – what is internal in us, physically and mentally, grows through its relationship to what is external. And the evidence of the Harvard Study and other research[7] suggests that this process does not end with childhood. Rather, our communication with other people, our external relationships, have a significant effect on the development of the internal world of our physical and mental health – and indeed our longevity – throughout our lives.

This points to the *group* level of human communication. We are intensely social, interdependent beings. We form naturally into groups because we depend on each other to meet a whole range of our fundamental needs – everything from providing the basics necessary to sustain life, to sharing the stories and ideas that give it meaning. In fact, we are so interdependent that one could say that most claims of independence are an illusion. For example, just think how many people are necessary to support the simple act of making a cup of tea.

Let's start with the tea-pickers. And the tea-processors and tea-packers. And all those involved in running the tea company – the managers, accountants, admin staff and so on. Then there's the transport chain – the truck drivers, train drivers and cargo shippers – and everyone involved in running those enterprises. And everyone who builds the trucks, trains and ships, and the different company infrastructures that support them. And everyone who builds and sustains the transport infrastructure – the roads, railways, ports, satellite systems (for weather forecasting, communications and navigation). Then add the retail infrastructure in the destination country. And the electricity infrastructure and everyone who supports all that. Ditto the water infrastructure. And the kettle manufacturers. And the cup makers. And teaspoon manufacturers. And the dairy farmers (or lemon growers). And everyone who's taught all of those people involved not just their specialist skills but also the basics needed for their jobs – reading, writing, numbers... And all those involved in simply getting everyone to work every day on public or private transport. And all of the people who build and run the computers and IT systems that underpin everything.

And why stop at the present? Why not include everyone in the past who's been involved? In the invention of electricity, say. Or the development of water treatment processes. Or in preparing the ground, and propagating and planting and nurturing the bushes on the tea estate. Or in pioneering the tea trade. Or developing banking, or money, reading, writing, numbers – and so on and so on and so on. By the time we actually fill the electric kettle with water, flick the switch and pop the teabag into the cup with a dash of milk or slice of lemon, it almost seems that half of humanity, back through history, might have been involved in some way in this process. And if you take sugar, even more. It's a minor miracle – and all for a cup of tea.

> **Come, let us have some tea and continue
> to talk about happy things**
> *Chaim Potok*[8]

The key point is that all of this is possible only because each separate human being involved is connected to at least one other human being – through communication. To put it another way, each relationship necessary for this system to work is the *result* of communication. Without communication, all the elements of the system would simply coexist as separate entities. No communication means no connection, no relationship, no network. And no cup of tea.

In short, it's the ability of people to communicate with one another that enables the group to cohere, endure and develop; and then, where it's thought to be advantageous, to merge with other groups, either through agreement or by force. Broadly speaking, this is how human society has developed since the appearance of *homo sapiens*. In fact, the very word 'communicate' derives from the Latin for 'to share' – *communicare* – which is related to the Latin word *communis*, meaning 'common', from which we get the English words 'community' and 'communal'. For the Romans, at least, the concept of the group was closely bound up with notions of what is embraced collectively (*communis*) and what is exchanged or circulated (*communicare*).

COMMUNICATION AND EVOLUTION

At the *species* level, human beings form the most socially complex groups in the animal world, and also have the most complex brains and the most advanced mental abilities. Evolutionary theory explains that the three things are inextricably linked – we have these complex brains and mental abilities thanks to the process of natural selection in the social environment, repeated over hundreds of thousands of years. Together, the combination has given human beings a huge evolutionary advantage over other creatures.

In other words, just as an individual will develop socially, physically, mentally and emotionally in response to their unique environment, so, as a species, we have evolved socially, physically, mentally and emotionally in response to a very wide range of different environments, over a very long period of time. For many thousands of years, as a species, we have been communicating with each other, learning from each other, cooperating with and challenging each other. There has been a constant back and forth, a sharing and sifting, of information – within individuals, between individuals, and within and between ever-larger groups of people – all of which has reached its current zenith with global telephony and the internet. In light of our species' fundamental need for communication, is it any wonder that there are now over five *billion* mobile phone users, more than two-thirds of the world's population? Or that the largest participatory organisation in the world is Facebook, with more than 2.2 billion active monthly users?[9] And given this sudden (and still growing) expansion in communication technology, is it any wonder that as a species we're struggling to use it consistently to create understanding between people? Another urgent reason for a talking revolution – worldwide – and an expanding cohort of talking revolutionaries to drive it.

In summary, putting together these three levels of the individual, the group and the species, you could say that we human beings don't just 'have' relationships – in a profound sense we *are* relationships. They're what define and shape us; what we're made of, both internally and externally. And it's the fundamental human need (and capacity) for communication, at every level, that keeps the whole ecosystem of our relationships functional. So much so, in fact, that 'communication' and 'relationship' could almost be seen as different terms for the same thing – human connection. Communication *is* relationship; relationship *is* communication – which is perhaps only a step away from saying that, at a profound level, we human beings *are* communication…

This is why conversation – ideally creative conversation – is so important. For just as muscles waste away if we don't exercise them, failing to engage in meaningful conversation can mean, in effect, that we're neglecting the vital internal and external relationships on which we depend for health and happiness. If we don't engage externally we can get flabby and weak internally. If we're not challenged enough by interacting with others we can get stuck and never grow. Thoughts and feelings can go around and around in our heads without ever being clearly expressed or discussed. Life can become smaller, harder and less fulfilling; more problematic and more isolated. And more miserable.

A PROBLEM *NOT* SHARED ... IS A PROBLEM DOUBLED?

For example, when we have a problem or disagreement with someone and fail (or refuse) to discuss it, effectively we then have two problems – the original problem *plus* a communication problem; and it's the latter that often causes most trouble. 'Why didn't you tell me?... You never listen! ... You just DON'T UNDERSTAND!' Relationships so often break down not because of the problems that come up but because of the way they're mishandled through poor – or no – communication.

Mike and Stella had been married for more than twenty years. Mike ran a small business in which Stella worked part-time, as she also looked after the house and their son, Alec, and did several sessions a week as a sports coach. When Alec became a teenager and more independent, Stella decided she wanted to develop her skills and get an academic degree, which she'd missed out on when she'd left school. But Mike said no. Her role in the family and the firm meant that it wasn't a good idea and things were fine as they were.

Stella was shocked and confused – she really hadn't expected this reaction – but things were made worse by Mike's behaviour. Rather than trying to understand Stella's needs and looking for a way forward, he did his best to avoid any conversation about what she wanted. Then, when cornered, he'd get angry, ridicule the idea, accuse Stella of being selfish and storm out.

So the original issue of Stella wanting to re-kindle her education, which could have been addressed by talking it through, escalated into the much bigger problem of Stella feeling she no longer had a mature, grown-up relationship with her husband – because they couldn't address something that really mattered to her. The longer this went on, the worse things got – till their marriage fell apart.

The situation probably sounds familiar. Our tendency to turn a problem into a crisis by failing to communicate in a way that seeks to meet the needs of those involved is around us everywhere – in couples, families, friendship groups, businesses, organisations large and small, governments, the international community; that is, wherever there are people.

The irony is that the technological revolution of the past twenty years has given us all kinds of channels through which to communicate; but, for all that, there hasn't been any kind of parallel advance in the 'humanware' of how we actually talk and listen to each other. The human side of the equation – our ability to share thoughts and feelings one-to-one, and to understand and engage with each other in real time to meet our mutual needs – is still as flawed and patchy as it ever was. If anything, in this age of the touch-screen, we seem in danger of losing touch with each other in any genuine sense, as we present partial or even false versions of ourselves online and project onto other people our imagined picture of what they are like. In other words, technology can provide connectivity but it takes real human beings to actually connect, to make and sustain meaningful human relationships, and to overcome differences.

By focusing on the needs that are common to all of us, creative conversation cuts to the heart of what it takes to build those relationships. The ability to talk about things is a freely available, non-digital capability that comes with us, pre-loaded. It's been developed through hundreds of thousands of years of human evolution to ensure our physical, mental and emotional survival; to enable us to grow in families, learn in groups, work in teams and live in societies. So, if we all have this almost miraculous in-built set of abilities, how can we use them better?

This brings us back to the question at the start of this chapter – 'If you want to have a long, happy and fulfilled life, how should you invest your time and effort *right now*?' The answer can be summed up in one sentence:

Seek to improve, as far as you can, the communication in **all** *of your existing and new relationships – through engaging in creative conversations.*

The first step in this process is to adopt the three fundamental principles of creative conversation explained in the next chapter.

Chapter 2

Three Principles of Creative Conversation

The Three Principles and the Three Practices of creative conversation are an example of 'the power of basics'. This is the idea that seeking to master the basics of any activity is what always brings the most benefit. It's an idea we all know – sort of – but which we tend to forget because, after learning the basics of something, we generally take them for granted. As a result, we often neglect them and in their place chase after something novel, or more 'sophisticated' or 'advanced'. The basics of dieting, for example, are 'input versus output' – if we burn and expel more calories than we consume we'll lose weight (and vice versa) - and yet a new diet fad seems to appear every year.

The Three Principles and the Three Practices together form the basics of creative conversation. Mastering any one of them will have a significant effect on our relationships. Mastering all six – and the art of conversation management that integrates them – will be transformative.

The Three Principles – Personal Responsibility, Openness and Creativity – express the *basic attitude or spirit* with which to approach creative conversation.

- *Personal responsibility* is essentially about our attitude to ourselves; it's about seeing ourselves as the active agent at the centre of things.

- *Openness* is essentially about our attitude to others and what they care about.
- And *Creativity* is essentially about our awareness of potential, about how every conversation contains the possibility to result in something of value.

Let's look at each of the Three Principles in more detail and then at how they relate to each other.

PERSONAL RESPONSIBILITY

The principle of personal responsibility is based on a simple observation – that we are each the central player in our own relationship/communication network. As a result, any changes we make in *our* behaviour can give any of our relationships a boost – maybe strengthening a friendship, ending an old feud or simply creating a better atmosphere – which can, in turn, affect our whole network. In the end, as with the 724 men in the Harvard Study, we all have a choice. Regardless of where we live, what we do, how much we earn or how things might have worked out in the past, we can all value our relationships with the people around us and invest in them – or not. Since the Harvard Study indicates what the positive return could be, making that investment seems a no-brainer.

So let's assume you want to make that investment – where do you start? And what does taking personal responsibility actually mean with regard to creative conversations?

To answer that, first think of someone who's easy to talk to. You might be partners, friends, colleagues, neighbours or family members – it doesn't matter. What matters is that you can talk to each other with honesty and respect, especially when things are a bit difficult.

Now, think of your conversations as a fibre optics cable linking the two of you, as shown (in cross-section) in Figure 2.1.

Figure 2.1 High bandwidth communication

It's got so much capacity it can accommodate arguments, misunderstandings and crises alongside all the warm, friendly stuff that also passes between you.

Communication like this has such 'high bandwidth' that everything you feed into it can be received and understood at the other end, while at the same time you're also receiving everything coming back loud and clear; and in the exchange you're creating fresh, mutual understanding that neither of you could have conjured individually. There's always a healthy amount of respect and consideration going back and forth; and if there's some friction or upset from time to time, the connection between you is resilient enough to keep the relationship intact. The communication – the sharing (*communicare*) – can still flow up and down along the cable.

Now think of the other end of the scale – someone you find really hard to talk to. This 'low bandwidth' communication is more like a piece of string between two tin cans (Figure 2.2). It's hard to hear each other. You say things but can't be sure if you've even been heard, let alone understood. Every conversation's a bit awkward, frustrating, even unpleasant, and if you had the choice you'd really rather not have it at all.

It could be said that all of our communication falls somewhere between these two extremes. You could live in the same house with someone and have low-bandwidth communication; or

Figure 2.2 Low bandwidth communication

you could see someone only every now and then and share consistently high-bandwidth communication.

Using this analogy, taking personal responsibility with regard to creative conversation means determining to expand the communication bandwidth of all the relationships you want to sustain and strengthen, wherever you can and as far as they can go. And in practical terms, this starts with understanding the current state of play of those relationships through mapping the relevant bandwidths.

Here's a simple way to do that.

On a piece of paper draw four concentric circles, with a dot in the middle to represent you (Figure 2.3). Starting from the outer ring, each circle represents Poor, OK, Good or Great relationships. Now, think of a group of people in your life and write their names in the appropriate circle. Then draw a line representing the 'communication bandwidth' between you and that person: the thicker the line, the greater the bandwidth.

What you should quickly see is that the farther the name is from the centre, the less bandwidth there is between you; that is, the less able you are to discuss things that matter to you both. In other words, *there is a close correlation between communication bandwidth and relationship 'distance', and one*

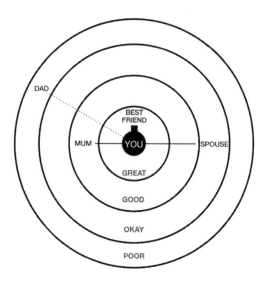

Figure 2.3 Communication bandwidth and relationship quality

tends to feed the other – the less easily you communicate, the more distant you are; the more distant you are, the less easily you communicate. As stated earlier, 'relationship' and 'communication' can be seen as different ways of expressing essentially the same thing – connection.

In Figure 2.3, for example, focused on 'your' immediate personal relationships, the closest is with your best friend – there's lots of bandwidth, as you can speak about *anything* together. You've got pretty good, two-way communication with your mum too. But with your spouse – well, there's a lot of stuff that's off-limits because talking about it just causes tension; it's tin-cans-on-a-string communication. And as for your dad – hardly any bandwidth at all, sadly. You've had some pretty bruising arguments in the past, so communication between you is sporadic and superficial, even though deep down you'd like it to be at least as good as with your mum. So he's on the outer ring, even though he and your mum live in the same house only a few streets from you.

From this perspective, taking personal responsibility means using creative conversation to move as many people as possible – or at least as many as one chooses – closer to the centre, so that more of our relationships can be like those of the Harvard Study men who lived longer, happier and healthier lives. And, of course, in making those relationships better for ourselves, we're doing the same thing for the other person too. Creative conversation doesn't mean having to spend a lot of time together or even having to like each other. It means that what is shared – *communicare* – adds value at both ends of the 'cable'. It's creative, in the broad sense of the word, because it meets one or more of our basic needs, which might be emotional, psychological or simply about the practical ins and outs of avoiding the misunderstandings, mistakes and confusion that can plague any area of our lives.

Tim needed an urgent operation to unclog an artery in his neck, but when he turned up for his hospital appointment, anxious to learn about the procedure, he was kept waiting. And waiting. And waiting.

By the time the consultant surgeon called him in he was fuming.

At once she apologised for his long wait – an emergency had suddenly diverted many of the hospital's staff, including her, and only now was she able to catch up on her scheduled work. She also warned that, thanks to the emergency, she might have to take a phone call to brief a colleague and hoped Tim wouldn't be offended by the interruption. 'Not at all,' said Tim, his anger evaporating as he realised the pressure she must have been under.

She then explained that the purpose of the meeting was to make sure he was clear about his diagnosis, to explain the options for treatment and, ideally, to make a decision there and then, as he was at that very moment at 'significant risk' of having a stroke.

The doctor then explained the surgical procedure, from beginning to end. She spoke kindly and in plain language, was easy to understand and answered all of Tim's questions. When the expected phone call came, she switched efficiently to briefing her colleague, again with great clarity. She then gave Tim her undivided attention for the remaining thirty minutes of the consultation.

Tim was impressed – not just by her medical expertise but by the clarity and consideration with which she addressed him. He felt respected, safe, confident and well informed. So impressed was he that he felt moved to share his experience with his local pharmacist while filling the prescription he'd been given.

'Ah, communication,' said the pharmacist. 'It's always that. We spend so much time in this shop dealing with misunderstandings, mistakes, customers not telling us the whole story. Dispensing drugs is the easy bit...'

Tim and his consultant have high-bandwidth communication, even though they don't really know each other. From the outset, the consultant takes responsibility for this creative conversation by seeking at every point to meet Tim's needs for reassurance (safety) and clarity. For example, sensing his anxiety, she shows empathy for his frustration at being kept waiting, explains the reason for the delay and warns him about the possible interruption. This is important because if we fail to acknowledge what the other person might be thinking or feeling the bandwidth can shrink at once, and the communication that follows might struggle to pass 'up and down the cable', both ways.

She then explains the structure of the discussion they are about to have – an important technique in helping others to understand – and, throughout, doesn't just focus on what she's 'transmitting' but also on what Tim is 'receiving'; that is, she makes sure that Tim fully understands what she's saying about his condition, his options for treatment and why he has to decide soon.

Creating the maximum possible bandwidth in all of our communication with other people, through creative conversations like this, is something we're all capable of. And it's not limited to just verbal communication. Our thoughts, words and deeds are inextricably linked, so we also communicate what we think about others through our actions. Sometimes a small, considerate gesture can say more about what we think than a thousand words; while behaviour – or even just the tone of our voice – that contradicts what we've communicated in words can destroy trust and, ultimately, relationships. In sum, creating maximum communication bandwidth demands that our thoughts, words and actions are consistent with each other.

Of course, expanding bandwidth isn't guaranteed to solve every problem we might have with people; that's not realistic. But it does give us the best possible shot at creating the conditions in which solutions can be discovered and explored.

PERSONAL RESPONSIBILITY IN A GROUP SETTING

This is true not just in intimate, personal relationships but in organisations large and small. Many professional and working relationships function really well, as in Tim's experience above, but there are also many that don't. Individually, those sub-functional relationships might not seem to matter very much but, collectively, they all have an effect on the health and performance of the organisation as a whole, for better or for worse.

To understand this better, here's another exercise. Draw a large circle on a sheet of paper. This represents any group of people you know well who interact regularly. It could be your family, friendship group, your colleagues at work, a sports team you play for; anything. Place dots at regular intervals around the circle to represent the people involved, including yourself, and name them. Now, how many one-to-one relationships are possible in that group? Draw a line between each pair of names and count them.[1] There are ten people in the example below (Figure 2.4), which means there are 45 possible relationships.

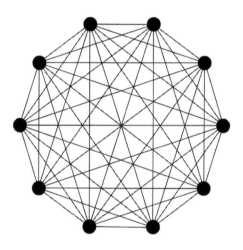

Figure 2.4 How many 1-2-1 relationships are possible in any group of people?

It doesn't take a maths wiz to realise that as more people are added to the group the number of possible relationships increases, except it's not in a linear fashion but *exponentially*. Doubling the number from ten to twenty people looks like this

(Figure 2.5) and more than *quadruples* the number of possible relationships to 190.

Figure 2.5 As more people are added to a group the number of possible relationships increases exponentially

This implies that the addition of even two or three positive (or negative) people to an organisation can have a far-reaching and apparently disproportionate effect. Ditto the improvement or deterioration of a few existing relationships. So, for a very practical and immediate reason, it's important to pay attention to this network of relationships by working to improve communication wherever possible.

Turning now to your diagram, draw lines that you think best represent the communication in *your* group, connecting everyone to everyone else. Use a thick, strong line to show resilient, open communication and thin lines, or even patchy, broken ones to show low-bandwidth communication. Guess if you're not sure – this is just an exercise. And remember that a thick line doesn't mean the individuals have to know each other well or be friends. It just means that they have high-bandwidth communication, even if it's on a purely working level.

Now, sit back and look at your diagram as a network. What does it show?

If your group is made up entirely of thick, robust lines you have something very precious – maximum communication and a network of strong, resilient relationships. You also have something highly unusual, because most relationship networks are a real dog's breakfast of good and bad, weak and strong; high, low and no bandwidth (Figure 2.6).

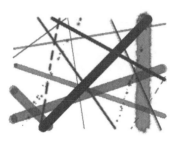

Figure 2.6 How strong is your human network?

Whatever the mix you're looking at, this is the human network of that group of people. Some of it's functioning at full potential, some of it's just ticking over; but some of it might really not be functioning well or even at all. So what effect does that have on that family, that group, that team or that organisation's performance as a whole?

If our electricity, plumbing and telephone network were in that subpar kind of state we'd probably be in the dark, up to our knees in water and unable even to call for help. But because this is a human network based on how we communicate with each other, we tend to accept its failings as just 'life' or maybe as too complex even to begin to fix. And even if we did want to do something about it, who would we call?

Well, the short answer is there's no one to call. The only person who can fix any particular human network is the person who *takes personal responsibility* and consciously decides to acknowledge their position at the centre of it – which in your case would be you.

Consider this situation, for example.

Figure 2.7 shows the relationship/communication network of *Kitchens4All* – a fictional kitchen design company in which 'You' are the Admin Assistant (although the principle works for any person or point on the circle, and for any group or family). Everyone in the company has a relationship with every other person but the quality of those relationships is pretty mixed, as shown by the different lines – very thick is great; thick is good; thin is OK and dotted is poor.

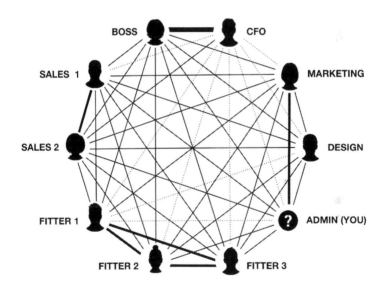

Figure 2.7 The relationship/communication network of *Kitchens4All*

Most of the relationships in *Kitchens4All* are 'OK' but there are clearly problems, the main one being the Chief Financial Officer (CFO), who doesn't seem to get on with anyone except the Boss – they're actually married – and one of the Sales staff.

'You' have a good relationship with a colleague who handles the marketing, but you find the CFO cold and pedantic, and you're barely on speaking terms with Fitter 1 – you had a blazing row a few weeks ago. The Fitters themselves are a tightknit crew, and the two Sales staff also get on well; but the Designer comes in every day, does the job and goes home without engaging with anyone except on strictly work terms.

Now, you could simply accept this network as it is – the company is stable, you get paid on time, nothing is unbearable and the bigger picture is, well, not your problem. Fair enough – just trundle on. OR you could take personal responsibility and decide to look at it like Figure 2.8.

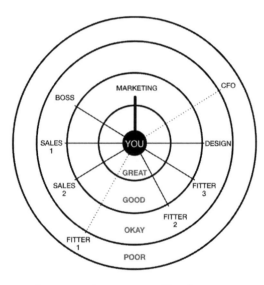

Figure 2.8: Putting yourself at the centre

Conceptually, you can always put yourself at the centre of any human network that includes you, however junior or peripheral you might think of yourself. And, practically, you take personal responsibility for your network *by trying to improve the communication in each of your relationships, through creative conversation.* Even a small improvement – so the CFO moves from 'Poor' to 'OK', say, or the Designer from 'OK' to 'Good' – can help change things for the better, both for your unique part of the network *and* for the network overall. Just imagine, for example, how much more satisfying your day-to-day working experience would be if Figure 2.8 looked more like Figure 2.9. By consciously working to improve the communication in each

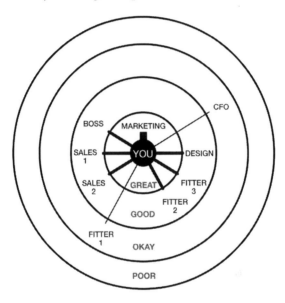

Figure 2.9 Improving your relationship/communication network relationships by one step – an individual perspective

of your relationships, they have all been upgraded. The result, individually, is not just that you personally enjoy work more since you get on better with everyone; collectively, it means that Figure 2.7 now looks like Figure 2.10.

The company still has weaknesses but the *entire* network has been strengthened, by just one person – 'You' – working to increase the communication 'bandwidth' within your own personal web of relationships. Remember, we're not talking

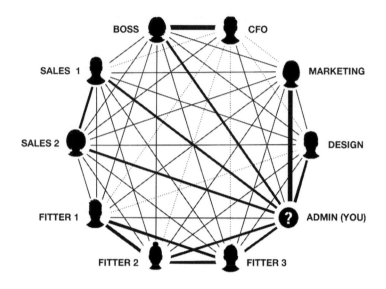

Figure 2.10 Improving your relationship/communication network relationships by one step – a group perspective

here about making Best Friends Forever (although you never know), but rather about creating the conditions between you and another person where *understanding can be increased to the greatest possible extent for that relationship at that time.* 'Understanding' is explored further in the next chapter, but it's important to remember that it does *not* mean agreeing - although it might lead to agreement.

With Fitter 1, for example, all you might be able to achieve is a situation where you're polite to each other and no more – but at least you're communicating every day. And maybe the Designer really doesn't want to talk about anything personal, but is happy to discuss ways in which your working interaction can be made more productive. So, different strokes for different folks – and by taking personal responsibility *you* can take the initiative for finding those right 'strokes'.

What's more, thanks to the principle of 'referent influence' explained earlier (pp. 4–5), your efforts are likely to galvanise others in the company, too, so the effects, in time, will multiply, strengthening the network further still. Some people will be encouraged by the small signs of improvement they see (or sense) and start acting more positively. Others might be curious that you managed to patch things up with Fitter 1, say, and ask you directly how you did it. You might even explain to one or two people the principles of creative conversation. In short, as you begin to change so your social environment will begin to reflect that change, directly or indirectly.

What's more, according to research led by the University of Pennsylvania's Annenberg School for Communication,[2] it needs only 25 per cent of people in a group to adopt a new social norm for a tipping-point to be reached where the whole group switches to the new norm. Which means that if you and only two others at *Kitchens4All* consistently practise creative conversation, the communication culture of the whole company will change for the better.

Of course, human relationships are always in flux and other factors will also be at play to counter this process. In families, for example, some negative relationships can seem as if cast in concrete. Even so, our steady efforts to improve communication in our relationships, using creative conversation, will *always* bring benefit in some way, either individually or collectively, or both.

'Sounds great. But we don't have time for all this talking. We're too busy.'

That's the reaction we got from a group of very hard-working school teachers in a socially deprived area of the UK. We were helping them find ways to have better conversations with hard-to-reach students and their families, so that life at their schools could be more productive.

43

Like many teachers, they were hugely overloaded, but much of the overload came from fire-fighting difficult, often tense, situations – crisis management. A typical conversation for them could be with a parent; but it might also include the Head, one or more students, social workers, educational psychologists and even police officers, any of whom might have a different interpretation of the facts, a different set of priorities or use different language to express themselves.

As we worked together the teachers came to realise that through the early application of creative conversation – and, crucially, through the understanding that came from it – they could create a calmer atmosphere, get to the heart of the matter more quickly and help develop better relationships for the future. At the end of our time together, one of them said, with some surprise, 'Compared to the time we spend dealing with misunderstanding, understanding takes no time at all!'

It was a pleasing result for us – but the teachers themselves had to instigate the change that followed. They each had to take personal responsibility. Each of them, individually, had to decide on the spirit in which they were going to conduct their conversations – day-to-day, hour-to-hour, minute-by-minute – rather than let the atmosphere be dictated by the often highly emotional state of others.

Those who took on this challenge later reported that they were now less inclined to make wrong assumptions, jump to easy conclusions or give instant advice, and were simply better at listening – to their students, their students' parents, and even their own family members. They were also doing less fire-fighting, as they were better at defusing tricky situations and getting to the root of problems before they escalated. As one teacher summed it up, 'Each conversation I have now is more effective; it has more value.'

Taking personal responsibility for any subpar human network of which we're a member might appear quite daunting, so it can help to remember a couple of things.

First, it's fundamentally an attitude we adopt, a frame of mind, which puts *us* in charge, regardless of status. Taking personal responsibility is telling oneself that 'I'm not going to wait for others to act – *I'm* going to take the bull by the horns and bring about change.' And, of course, we don't have to announce this to anyone – we can just make the decision and do it.

The second thing to remember is that the 'it' we do can be whatever we choose. Let's say that the really tough nut to crack in *Kitchens4All* is the CFO. You could decide that, from now on, you'll begin every interaction between the two of you with a cheerful smile. It's a small thing, it's entirely in your power – and yet it could be the start of gradually warming up, opening up, that relationship. Or you could decide that you're going to practise and develop your creative conversation skills with someone less challenging – the Designer, say, or the Boss – and only then tackle the CFO.

In other words, we can start with small things and/or easier people and work up to the more difficult stuff step-by-step, as our confidence grows, in a way and at a pace we're comfortable with. Along the way we might also adopt a zero-tolerance attitude to misunderstanding, whether we're 'transmitting' or 'receiving', and make it our mission to end every encounter at a point where we've both understood and been understood. So taking personal responsibility means taking charge *on our terms*. It's actually very empowering.

> **How do you eat an elephant? One mouthful at a time.**
> *African proverb.*

It's also very important to understand that taking personal responsibility means taking responsibility for *our* side of the equation, too; that is, our own thoughts, feelings, words, tone and actions.

This is essential because it's a human tendency to externalise what is actually internal - to blame, point the finger, accuse. We say 'He makes me *so* angry!' when 'he' is simply behaving in a way that we don't like. More accurate would be to say 'When he does that *I* get so angry!' It might sound like a small difference but this phrasing switches the focus of responsibility through 180 degrees. If we say 'He makes me *so* angry!' the responsibility is his - therefore *he* needs to change. Paradoxically, this also gives away our power - unless he changes we will remain angry and just seethe impotently. Whereas if we say 'When he does that *I* get so angry!' the responsibility for how we feel rests with us - and also empowers us. We might still want him to change his behaviour or attitude but we are at least aware that some - or maybe all - of the problem lies with our own thoughts, feelings, words and actions, which we have the power to change if we choose to.

In fact, a growing self-awareness is both a cause and an effect of taking personal responsibility for expanding our communication bandwidth with other people, which leads us into the second fundamental principle - openness.

So just to recap...

To take *personal responsibility* includes:

- consciously acknowledging that we are at the centre of any of our networks of human relationships and that our thoughts, words and deeds are always affecting in some way the individuals in them
- deciding to increase the communication bandwidth of some or all of those relationships, privately if we wish, and at our own pace

- understanding that our thoughts, words and deeds are inextricably linked, so we also communicate what we think about others through our actions
- taking ownership of our own thoughts and feelings, not attributing responsibility (or blame) for them elsewhere

OPENNESS

An attitude or spirit of openness in creative conversation is expressed in two basic questions – who are we prepared to talk to and about what?

Starting with 'Who?', it's all-too-easy to think that some people are worth talking to and others are not. Appearance, age, status, culture or a whole host of other less obvious factors can prompt us to feel more comfortable talking to this person rather than that person. It's natural, normal, and our brains have evolved that way for good reason – to band together with 'friends' against 'foes' and other challenges, for evolutionary advantage. But it's also a huge restriction that we impose on ourselves because we are, in effect, denying the potential benefits that can come from engaging with a wide variety of people in a meaningful way; benefits like company, friendship, support, collaboration, solutions to problems, shoulders to cry on and people simply to enjoy life with. Indeed, there's evidence that interacting with a range of different people is as important to the individual as maintaining a varied, balanced diet.[3] Not only does it generally make us less susceptible to social prejudice and polarisation, it also tends to make us work harder at achieving consensus, more innovative and better at solving complex problems.

Openness has advantages at the group level, too. The communication bandwidth of each different relationship between individuals in the group might vary but in one respect they're all equal. Everyone in the group has their own unique experience, viewpoint and feelings about things common to that group, *and so the group will be healthy and strong to the degree that all those views and feelings are heard and the underlying needs addressed.* The group as a whole knows, collectively, all sorts of things that are relevant to it but it takes an attitude of openness to bring everything out and make it all known, so that relationships can be strengthened and the group can thrive. In fact, if it doesn't adopt this attitude, it's a sure bet that in time the group will stagnate or even eventually die – of ignorance, unfulfilled potential, groupthink or any of the common maladies that afflict organisations across the globe every day.

The same dynamics can also be seen at the level of society and history is full of examples. Societies dominated by systems of thought that accept or reject ideas according to a rigid dogma might flourish for a while but over time filter out the very things they need to respond positively to new challenges. The Communist USSR and its East European satellites spring to mind as recent examples.

> **If there is a storehouse of treasures but no key, then it cannot be opened, and if it cannot be opened, then the treasures inside cannot be seen.**
> *Nichiren*[4]

Whether the benefit is initially sought on an individual or collective level, a first step to developing more openness towards other people can be to become aware of our own personal tendencies. When and why, at key moments, do we open up to some people and close down to others? Is it how we've been brought up? Is it about status or culture? Is it the situation or something inherent in us, such as shyness? To put it more directly, in deciding how open or closed we're going to be, which of our basic needs are involved?

NEEDS AND VALUES

This can be a tricky question to answer, as our needs jostle for our attention. They compete with each other, complement each other and can even contradict each other. To further complicate the picture, the relationship between our needs and the emotions we attach to them is not always obvious, especially to ourselves. For example, fear is a response triggered by a threat to our need for safety, but it's often expressed as anger. How many of us recognise that dynamic, though, and how might we think, speak and act differently if we did?'

One way to understand ourselves better is to recognise that the needs we feel are most important to us form the basis of our *values*. As the word suggests, these are things we value - we care about - and so carry for us a powerful emotional charge. But because values are part of the fabric of our emotional lives we can often be aware of them only when we sense, rightly or wrongly, that they're being abused in some way.

- *'I didn't like the disrespectful way he spoke to me.'*
- *'That's not fair.'*
- *'I just don't trust them.'*

So in deciding how open or closed we're going to be in any encounter, we might ask ourselves which of our values are involved (and Appendix A might help again here). For example, do we most value connection – or privacy? Are they in competition? Is another need altogether in the mix – or several? Once we become more keenly aware of how and why we react to different people in different settings, based on our understanding of our own needs and values, we can start to challenge ourselves to think and behave in other ways.

The second step, then, can be to *make a conscious decision* to adopt, as a default, an attitude of openness and non-discrimination towards other people. Whether we then act on this decision gradually – by letting people into our 'circle of acceptance' bit by bit – or with a 'big bang' is up to us.

Eva decided to celebrate her thirtieth birthday by booking a cruise to St Petersburg. It would swing by Oslo, Copenhagen and Tallin on the way out, pop into Helsinki on the way back – and was going to be great. Except for one thing – Eva would be alone.

'Not alone-alone,' she explained, 'because it was a package tour and of course there'd be other people on it. But I didn't have anyone to go with – which was a real wake-up call for me. I'd reached 30 and I realised I was not in a very good place. I was in a not well-paid job that I really didn't like, I had a small flat and a small circle of friends – and that was about it. And I already had a failed marriage behind me. I'd thought of myself as an attractive, intelligent person – I'd got a good degree from a good university – but actually my life had shrunk.

'Looking back – and it embarrasses me to say this – it was because I was so arrogant. I was critical of everyone. That's why I had so few friends, and it's probably why my marriage broke up too. No one could meet my ridiculous standards – what they thought, how they spoke, what they wore; nothing was good enough, basically. But when I realised that there was no one to go on the cruise with me – actually, that no one wanted *to go with me – that was painful.*

'So on that trip I made a simple rule – I wouldn't choose who I spoke to. I would suspend all my judgmental thoughts and sit in the first free seat in the restaurant or on the sightseeing trips, and just talk to whoever I found myself next to. No

matter who they were, what they looked like, where they were from – bang, no judgment. I'd talk to them.

'And it was a revelation. It was fantastic. I had so many great conversations. Not every time but close. There were a couple of women I remember in particular – middle-aged, quite ordinary-looking, they went everywhere together. In the past I wouldn't have given them a second glance, but one of them was a professor of philosophy at UCL and the other was a professional painter. They were old friends and ran away from their husbands once a year on a foreign trip – they'd been around the world together. They were so interesting – and I'd never have known if I hadn't made that rule about not choosing who I spoke to. I was so surprised. And more than once I had conversations with people that almost left me in tears when I heard their life stories about what they'd been through, good and bad.

'And people were interested in me, too, which I found odd – talking to strangers about myself. But that was part of the bargain I made before I left – I couldn't just take; I had to give as well.

'Anyway, it all had a deep effect on me. I came back a changed woman, changed my job – changed everything really, bit by bit.'

This open, non-discriminating investment in relationships, old and new, is very egalitarian. It treats people with respect, regardless of who they are, what they own, where they come from – or what they think or believe. But, let's be honest – it can also be a real challenge. A spirit of openness means, inevitably, that we'll hear and have to deal with stuff we don't like. Personal criticism, offensive attitudes, unpleasant opinions – the world is full of views we'd rather avoid.

This brings us to the 'What?' question. What are we prepared to talk about – not just in general, but with *this* particular person?

Well, we are, of course, completely free to choose not to engage in or to end any conversation that crosses our personal red lines. And certainly nothing advocated in these pages says anyone has to put up with abuse of any sort. Even so, at times it takes courage to be open enough to listen to what makes us uncomfortable and to really try to understand where it's coming from. It by no means follows that we have to accept what we've heard, but any challenge we want to make will be that much stronger if it's delivered from a position of understanding rather than simply as a knee-jerk rejection. But why is it, when a conversation strays into no-go areas or transgresses our values, that almost as an instinctive reflex we find ourselves closing off from the other person, or even getting angry?

The answer is that our basic needs are so powerful that, whether we're conscious of them or not, we move (physically, mentally, emotionally) towards people, relationships, situations and environments that we think will meet them and away from those that don't – and we suffer if we get stuck. Think how painful it can be, for instance, when we are forced to listen impotently to a verbal attack on something we value or someone we really care about. A whole range of our needs might be under threat – for fairness, accuracy, expression (we can't answer back), power, influence, safety (for ourselves or those we care about) and so on – and we agonise because we can't do anything to meet those needs in that moment, except maybe shout at the tv or radio, or post a snarky comment online.

In fact, a threat to, or denial of, any of our basic needs will always cause some degree of conflict – between individuals, groups and/or *within* the individual. For example, we might literally fight others for the right to express our identity (we have a basic need to be acknowledged and accepted); or we might choose to hide our identity – for fear of persecution, say (we also have a basic need for safety); but then we might be conflicted *internally* with feelings of cowardice or lack of integrity. So when push comes to shove, in one way or another our dominant needs and values override all other considerations – which might even include close relationships, let alone those that aren't so close.

Musician Marqus was telling his friend Leon about a conversation he'd had the day before with a mate, Danny the drummer, during a break in rehearsals. Marqus had been surprised – appalled, in fact – at Danny's political views, which he recounted to Leon at great, disapproving length.

'I was getting really wound up,' said Marqus, 'But after a bit I thought, "Stuff this" and just walked off.'

'Whoa. Why?' It was Leon's turn to be surprised.

'You kidding me?' said Marqus. 'I thought I knew Danny, but it was like, well, I didn't. Suddenly it's like he's a stranger, like we're on different planets almost. And the stuff he was saying… We were never going to agree, so what's the point?'

'In talking?'

'Yeah.'

Leon looked bothered. 'Well, how's anyone ever going to change their mind, or even just think differently about stuff, if they block out what they don't want to hear? Or only ever talk to people who basically agree with them.'

Marqus shrugged.

'*So you never asked him* why?'

'*Why what?*'

'*Why he's got those views? I mean, he is a mate.*'

'Was,' *said Marqus.*

This exchange is a typical example of polarisation. It happens all the time – with family members, friends, colleagues, people we hardly know, people on Twitter and Facebook – and the pattern is pretty standard. In this case, Marqus clearly felt that something he cares about – a *value* related ultimately to one or more of his basic needs – was being threatened or denied by Danny's political views, so after a bit of verbal argy-bargy he withdrew. If we heard Danny's side of the story he might very well say the same about Marqus's political views – and might even have been on the point of walking away himself. In fact, polarisation can be seen as a form of instinctive conflict management, where those involved sense that continued contact might lead to further escalation, even violence. Walking away, literally or metaphorically, is mutual protection – which might be necessary in the heat of the moment but all too often it also closes down the possibility for further conversation. Communication bandwidth shrinks (if only on that particular subject), the relationship deteriorates and a new norm of 'closedness', fuelled by mutual hostility, rules the day. And the next day. And the next. Which can turn into weeks, months, years, decades – even centuries – as the words and actions of the other person (or group) are routinely interpreted to prove just how awful they truly are.

THE POWER OF 'CORE BELIEFS'

Polarisation becomes especially intense if a 'core belief' is involved on one side or the other (or, most difficult, both). A core belief – also called a 'sacred value', 'object of devotion' or 'object of veneration' – can be broadly interpreted as what we base our lives on, consciously or unconsciously, to give it meaning. It's similar to what Stephen Covey[5] calls *centers*.

> Each of us has a center, though we usually don't recognize it as such. Neither do we recognize the all-encompassing effects of that center on every aspect of our lives.[6]

A core belief is formed when the basic needs we most value become attached to a specific goal, person, activity or object, real or abstract. Common examples are a loved one, the family, the nation, one's work and a belief system (political or religious), any of which can bundle together several values and satisfy a number of strong needs. For example, a core belief in the family can meet our needs for affection, acceptance, understanding, community, safety, stability, growth, nurturance, stimulation and play and can embody such values as loyalty, pride and tolerance - the list is long.

The bottom line is that our core belief exercises a powerful hold on us. All individuals and groups have a core belief, which is also the basis of individual and group identity and morality; for example, we might never condone violence – except to protect our core belief. And as long as we think that our core belief is within reach, we'll draw strength and inspiration from it. The picture of our family or loved one in time of stress, the nation's flag raised on the battlefield, the religious or political symbol we wear or carry with us everywhere we go – all are day-to-day examples of the motivational power of a core belief. The relationship between our needs, values and core belief is shown in Figure 2.11.

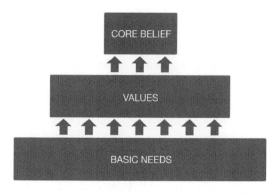

Figure 2.11 How our individual needs are expressed in our values and core belief

It's precisely because our core belief is so central to our lives that losing it leads to confusion, suffering, decline and even death. It's a like a compass, a central reference point that helps us make decisions as we navigate through daily life. Without it we can quickly get lost, like the sports star whose career comes to an end and turns to drink or drugs to fill the vacuum, or someone who loses the will to carry on when their beloved partner dies. Small wonder, then, that a threat to (or denial of) our core belief is the most serious of all challenges, which is why we're so thin-skinned when it happens and why core beliefs can be at the heart of the most intense, polarised and protracted conflicts.[7] 'No surrender, no compromise – [*core belief here*] or death!'

Put simply, the more justified we feel, especially if a core belief is involved, the more entrenched our 'closedness' tends to become. We dig in our heels over who we will and won't talk to; or what we will and won't talk about; or usually both, since the unacceptable person and the unacceptable opinion often merges in a single unit of, well, unacceptableness. And increasingly, we surround ourselves with an echo-chamber of likeminded souls, both offline and on, that reinforces what we think and feel, even in the face of evidence that contradicts it. This is because, says cognitive neuroscientist Tali Sharot, 'Seeking out and interpreting data in a way that strengthens our pre-established opinions is known as the "confirmation bias". It is one of the strongest biases humans hold.'[8] Indeed, research suggests that it might even be hardwired in our brains.[9] Social media can therefore simultaneously connect us to more and more people and, paradoxically, increasingly isolate us in a highly particular and limited worldview. Birds of a feather flock together – and the online world simply magnifies this, especially where strong feelings are involved. As the psychologist Molly Crockett has noted:[10]

> …there is a serious risk that moral outrage in the digital age will deepen social divides. A recent study suggests a desire to punish others makes them seem less human. Thus, if digital media exacerbates moral outrage, in doing so it may increase social polarization by further dehumanizing the targets of outrage. Polarization in the US is accelerating at an alarming pace, with widespread and growing declines in trust and social capital. If digital media accelerates this process further still, we ignore it at our peril…
>
> Digital media may promote the expression of moral outrage by magnifying its triggers, reducing its personal costs and amplifying its personal benefits. At the same time, online social networks may diminish the social benefits of outrage by reducing the likelihood that norm-enforcing messages reach their targets, and could even impose new social costs by increasing polarization.

The irony is that when we wholly externalise an issue – 'It's *them*, out there; *they're* the problem' – we not only fail to overcome it (by giving away our power to change the situation) but we can harm ourselves in the process. As we've seen, the Harvard Study identifies that holding grudges against others is a deeply unhealthy, unhelpful, life-sapping habit – it's a form of sustained hostility, which always comes at a cost of some kind. So the longer a grudge is held, the more damaging the effect on the person (or group) who holds it.

However, as recent political history shows – in Northern Ireland and South Africa, for example – talking conducted in a spirit of openness can reverse this process. It can achieve outcomes that violence, silence and shunning simply can't, no matter how justified those approaches might seem. But sustaining the spirit of openness takes conscious, committed effort to counter our natural reflex to close up whenever we sense that our basic needs (and/or our values and/or our core belief) are being blocked or threatened. The spirit of openness recognises that people, their opinions – *our* opinions – can change. But rarely in one conversation. It also recognises that they – and we – might never change.

Creative conversation isn't primarily about that though. It's primarily about connection and understanding; about improving the communication by which change *might* come – if those involved choose it.

So, practically, a spirit of openness is expressed in the willingness – at least for a while – to put our opinions to one side; to suspend judgment; to give others the benefit of the doubt; and not to blame, criticise or find fault.

Nothing human is alien to me.
Terence[11]

Ultimately, it takes openness sustained over a period of time to build (or rebuild) relationships; to look for nuance in the views of those we disagree with and to represent them with accuracy; to understand the human needs underlying the thoughts and actions of other people – and our own; to entertain the possibility that we ourselves might (have to) change; and to constantly seek to expand communication bandwidth between 'us' and 'them' so there is resilience in our relationships, even where there is disagreement.

So rather than expending a lot of time and energy trying to change someone's mind, it might be more useful for us to put that effort into remaining open and trying to understand why they think as they do. How then to challenge them in a way that supports and maintains the openness that is vital to creative conversation is explored in depth in Chapter 4. Once mastered, it can lead to valuable, even extraordinary, insights, especially from interactions with people who would normally be outside our comfort zones.

So just to recap...

To adopt an attitude of *openness* includes:

- expanding the circle of who we are prepared to talk to and about what
- recognising the benefits of openness individually, to the group and to society as a whole – for growth, development, resilience and problem-solving
- understanding that we open up when our needs are met and our values and core beliefs are respected – and we close down when they are not
- putting our judgmental thoughts and responses on hold, even if only temporarily, but also being prepared to self-reflect and embrace personal change

CREATIVITY

If taking *personal responsibility* puts us in the driving seat of our own, unique communications network, and *openness* unlocks the no-go areas of who we feel we can speak to and about what, the third of the Three Principles – *creativity* – is our approach to handling the twists and turns of conversation.

As with driving a vehicle, this requires focus, effort and a desire to get somewhere. But what does 'getting somewhere' mean? And what exactly is being created?

As mentioned earlier, creativity in this context is rooted in the awareness of potential; in the spirit to try to produce something of value from every conversation, however brief it might be, *through addressing the basic needs of those involved.* This spirit of creativity has to be quite robust – stubborn, even – as our needs are often expressed in a negative form precisely because they're *not* being met. This was one of the great insights of Marshall Rosenberg,[12] the founder of 'nonviolent communication':

> Judgments, criticisms, diagnoses and interpretations of others are all alienated expressions of our needs. If someone says 'You never understand me', they are really telling us that their need to be understood is not being fulfilled. If a wife says 'You've been working late every night this week; you love your work more than you love me', she is saying that her need for intimacy is not being met.[13]

To 'hear' the need in a complaint or criticism or verbal attack isn't easy; for some people, it seems almost intolerable, ridiculous even. But it is most certainly doable and learnable, using the spirit of openness discussed above and the practical actions explained in the following chapters. To then address that need positively – to take a lemon and make lemonade – demands the spirit of creativity, the desire to create 'something of value' by giving the situation all we've got in the present moment. We may be discussing the past or the future, but the way we invest our efforts in this present moment determines that outcome.

Often, this 'something of value' is limited simply to *connection* with another human being. It's such a basic need that many of us probably take it for granted – although that doesn't mean we necessarily do the right things to satisfy it.

Complaining and criticising usually close people down, for example, and push them away. And as we saw in Chapter 1, isolation, unless it's consciously chosen, is not good for us. So creating a connection with another person through talking and listening, even fleetingly and even if we disagree with them, can be hugely valuable in itself. It's a way of acknowledging that person's existence, that 'You're there and you count for something', which sometimes is all that's needed to break down the invisible prison that surrounds someone.

Once a connection is made, or if one already exists, something else is created with each conversation – *possibility*. A door opens on the chance to fashion something unique and new and valuable, in that moment, limited only by our imagination and skill. Dialogue has been described as 'thinking together'[14] and 'interthinking'[15] – a form of interaction that creates a 'safe space' in which we can express emotions, explore ideas, examine options and work out solutions (co-create) without fear of negative judgment. It's like having the confidence to put our cards on a large table, whatever they are and however half-formed they might be, so that we can look at them together, in a positive way, and decide what's of value, what isn't, and what might now be done. So creativity also implies openness – the willingness to 'park' our own opinions and critical judgments and, if necessary, let go of them entirely. This in turn implies being prepared to be changed ourselves by what we hear, which can create new horizons for us, too.

With possibility comes another huge 'something of value' that can be created through conversation – *hope*. Sometimes it will spark into being through learning something we didn't know – we were in despair because a situation seemed hopeless but now, with this new piece of information, perhaps a solution, a way through, might be found. But sometimes the hope will ignite not because of anything specific we might learn but simply because the person with whom we're having that conversation inspires us. Their attitude, their way of thinking, their spirit cuts through our gloom – like the sun shining through clouds – and we think, 'Well, maybe I can win after all. Somehow...' Creating hope is a wonderful skill to develop.

Perhaps the most important possibility that we can create through conversation is that of *understanding*. This has different levels. On one level, through 'thinking together' we can create *clarity* from confusion, intellectually and emotionally. Helping another person to explain what they think and feel can encourage them to be more precise and nuanced about their thoughts and emotions, to the point that they might even have a great moment of realisation, often about their needs or values or goals. And they can do the same for us, of course.

It's ironic that, in these days of non-stop, almost universal communication, clarity can be harder than ever to come by, simply because we have so much (often conflicting) information on tap. Clarity demands that we cut through the 'noise' of information and focus on the way we process what we're hearing, moment by moment. But it's a prize that needs to be worked for, through the way we understand others, the way we express ourselves in return and the way we challenge everyone's thinking, including our own.

> **If you want to go fast, go alone.**
> **If you want to go far, go with others.**
> *African proverb*

On a deeper level than achieving clarity about what we think and feel – vital as this is – most of us have the basic need to be *understood*. In fact, it seems almost to be in our genes, as social animals, that we are each acknowledged, understood, accepted and appreciated by our group, however we might define it – family, friends, colleagues, society – for this is how we belong. It's largely from these relationships that we create meaning for ourselves, which is why they are so central to our well-being and longevity.

Late one Saturday afternoon Eshan found himself in the vet's busy waiting-room, watching the clock tick towards six. His cat, Buddy, was due for his annual check-up but the vet was running late. Eshan sighed, irritated. He had better things to do with his time and the scratches on his arm were starting to really sting – Buddy had put up quite a fight getting into the pet-carrier that was now resting on Eshan's lap.

'Is it anything serious?'

The question came from a plump young woman sitting two seats away. She nodded to Buddy. On the seat between them was a moggy in a wire cage – hers.

'No, just routine.'

Eshan smiled briefly and looked away. Making small talk with strangers didn't come easily. But something in the young woman's expression – a hint of anxiety – made him turn back.

'How about you?'

'Ah, Well. Cat cancer, I'm afraid.'

'Oh, I'm sorry. Is it…?'

'Yes. I think it's the end of the line.'

And so began a twenty-minute conversation about their cats, and the role that pets had played in their lives, and mortality, and how to cope with loss. Then the vet appeared and Eshan took Buddy in for his brief examination. When they came back out into the waiting-room the young woman and her moggy were alone. She smiled bravely.

'Last in the queue.'

Eshan swallowed hard, almost in tears. 'Look, I really hope – '

The young woman shook her head. 'No, no, you've been really kind. Thank you so much. Thank you for talking to me.'

She got to her feet, picked up the wire cage, and went through to the vet.

This was a creative conversation. It didn't last long, nothing was solved, the sick cat was put to sleep – and yet something of value was created between Eshan and the young woman. She was able to express her sadness and her fear, but also her love and appreciation for her animal. And she was also able to get a glimpse of her life beyond this intense moment. In turning back and asking that simple question – 'How about you?' – and then engaging fully in their exchange, Eshan had created the opportunity for her to do all that and, crucially, for her not to feel alone in her suffering. A small deed but a good deed. They never saw each other again – but Eshan never forgot the experience. Despite his initial reluctance, he'd transformed a boring, irritating wait into something of value by meeting the young woman's needs – for connection, expression, hope, understanding, appreciation and maybe more. And in seeing how a conversation can move from low to high bandwidth, perhaps 'small talk with strangers' now comes a bit more easily to him.

To grasp the potential power of creativity in our conversations, just imagine the opposite – non-creativity or, worse, destructiveness. Sadly, it's the reality of many of our day-to-day exchanges. Table 2.1 shows how a creative approach compares to a non-creative one.

The table is far from exhaustive – much can probably be added to both columns. But picture the difference if Eshan had at any point in his conversation with the young woman employed any of the attitudes in the right-hand column. And yet we probably do one or more of these every day with someone; often – alas – with those closest to us.

Table 2.1 Creative and non-creative attitudes and actions

CREATIVITY...	NON-CREATIVITY...
Empathises	Distances, judges, condemns
Clarifies	Confuses, obscures, misrepresents
Explores	Lacks curiosity, ignores, withdraws
Opens up	Closes down, defends, denies
Conveys respect	Belittles, insults, mocks
Seizes the moment, takes a chance	Plays it safe, kills spontaneity
Offers ideas and suggestions	Rejects ideas, insists on only one way
Challenges	Argues, attacks – or accepts defeat
Helps others talk	Dominates, doesn't listen
Reflects	Is blinkered
Is flexible	Is inflexible, stubborn
Develops mutual understanding	Misinterprets, misleads, creates antipathy
Focuses on what's being said	Goes off on an irrelevant tangent
Collaborates, seeks a 'win-win' outcome	Competes, tries to win
Gets to the heart of things	Misses the point
Takes responsibility	Excuses, blames, avoids
Creates trust	Creates mistrust, doubt

Two attitudes in the 'creativity' column merit a little more attention at this point – respect and trust.

First, it's easy to talk about the importance of respect and how crucial it is to any relationship but how do we actually show it? Respect doesn't just arise of its own accord. It has to be earned. It has to be created. One very effective way of doing this is to give someone else the gift of our time and non-judgmental attention. This relates back to the discussion of openness. Striving to understand how the other person sees things and respecting their right to their view, whether we agree with it or not, can create even more bandwidth in a relationship than always seeing eye to eye. In other words, adopting respect as a default position at the start of a conversation can be a powerful tool to create more *mutual* respect as a result of the conversation.

Second, trust is a quality that is usually created over time, incrementally, and deepens as words are matched with actions. Like respect, trust has to be earned. It is often hard won and easily lost – but what does it really mean to trust someone?

Researchers at the Canadian military think-tank have identified[16] four distinct but associated elements in trust – competence, benevolence, integrity and predictability. *Competence* relates to our confidence that someone can successfully complete a particular task. *Benevolence* relates to our belief that someone cares about our well-being. *Integrity* relates to our judgment that someone shares the same values as us, in the same context. And *predictability* means that we are confident that someone will act in a way that is consistent with one or more of the other three elements. We have complete trust in another person (or group of people) when they tick all four boxes – but often they don't.

For example, we might judge that someone cares about us (benevolence) and shares our values (integrity) but for one reason or another think they can't deliver – they might not be up to it (competence) or perhaps they've let us down in the past (predictability). On the other hand, someone might be very good at what they do (competence) but, when push comes to shove, will they really come through for us (benevolence)?

Creating trust is a key element in expanding the bandwidth of our communication with others and these four elements can be useful in pinpointing where it's strong and where it might need more work. Because, very simply, the more we trust someone, the more we will share with them and vice versa – and the more resilient our relationship will be.

So just to recap...

Creativity involves:

- understanding that every exchange is unique and that 'something of value' can be created through meeting the basic needs of those involved
- seeking above all to create connection, through which – amongst other things – understanding, hope, trust and respect might also be created
- conveying respect through giving the other person your time and full attention
- seeking to build trust through persistently demonstrating competence, benevolence, integrity and predictability

THE THREE PRINCIPLES WORK TOGETHER – AND WITH THE THREE PRACTICES

These, then, are the Three Principles that support creative conversation and the talking revolution – taking *personal responsibility* for working to improve communication in our unique network of relationships; progressively expanding it by embracing an attitude of *openness*; and developing our *creativity* by adopting, more and more, the attitudes and actions in the left-hand column of Table 2.1 and discarding those in the right-hand column. As might be expected, the principles work in tandem (Figure 2.12).

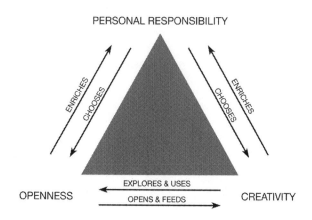

PERSONAL RESPONSIBILITY

ENRICHES / CHOOSES

ENRICHES / CHOOSES

EXPLORES & USES

OPENS & FEEDS

OPENNESS   CREATIVITY

Figure 2.12 How the Three Principles relate to each other.

By taking personal responsibility to use openness and creativity in how we communicate, our lives are enriched and our well-being and longevity enhanced. And by choosing an inclusive, non-discriminating approach to communication we open up many more possibilities for our creativity, which is then free to explore and develop this wider range of options. In short, creative conversation is win-win, for ourselves and others.

Simple.

Or is it? Maybe this all sounds a bit, well, idealistic. Nice in theory but not of the real world.

Well, yes and no. On the 'yes' side of the balance, the reality is that the more we care about something and the more emotion we invest in it, the harder creative conversation tends to become. This is because, as we saw in the discussion on openness, when we care about something we tend to become more protective of it; we are sensitive to threats – real or perceived – and so staying out of the right-hand column in Table 2.1 becomes increasingly difficult. If we're being criticised or something we cherish is being attacked in some way, the natural response is to close up or withdraw, to become defensive or counter-attack, or to find some other way to deflect the blow. The Three Principles go out of the window and non-creative or even destructive conversation takes its place.

On the 'no' side, this is why it's so important that the Three Principles of creative conversation are supported by, and expressed through, the *Three Practices* of Understanding, Being Understood and Challenging. By developing the habit of using these for *all* our interactions, large and small, we can even get to the point of employing creative conversation when we're under the hammer of severe criticism or our most deeply held views are being abused.

So let's now explore the Three Practices in detail.

Part Two

Three Practices of Creative Conversation

Part Two devotes a chapter to each of the three practical skills of creative conversation.

Chapter 3: Understanding stresses how important it is to make striving to understand the other person our starting-point in any conversation and offers various practical skills to help develop this habit.

Chapter 4: Challenging explores how we can challenge others in ways that produce positive rather than negative results.

Chapter 5: Being Understood explains how, by focusing on the needs of the listener, we can maximise our chances of being fully and properly heard ourselves.

If the Three Principles express the *basic attitude or spirit* with which to approach creative conversation, the Three Practices – Understanding, Challenging and Being Understood – are the *basic actions* through which we can apply this spirit in our everyday exchanges with other people.

Ways of nurturing, sustaining and repairing relationships through conversation have been known about for years in the world of psychotherapy. They just haven't been broadly applied in the wider world where they're so sorely needed. Much of the thinking behind the Three Practices stems from the work of Carl Rogers, generally regarded as the father of modern person-centred psychotherapy, and psychologist Gerard Egan. Rogers pioneered ways of interacting with others in ways they found helpful, based on positive self-regard and empathy. He famously didn't give advice, preferring to talk to people in a way that helped them understand and challenge their own thinking, and to identify their own solutions. He also understood that the way in which we listen to other people has a huge bearing on how they talk to us, and that 'conventional listening' is flawed in its ability to get to the heart of things. 'Most people do not listen to understand,' he said. 'They listen to reply.' Building on Rogers' work, Egan went on to write *The Skilled Helper*,[1] which since its publication in 1975 has become a standard text for those wanting to develop counselling skills.

In essence, the Three Practices are rooted in the tried and tested insights of Rogers and Egan, and adapted to the demands of everyday conversation in the wider world; for, as Sherry Turkle[2] has noted, 'The psychoanalytic tradition deepens the culture of conversation because it demonstrates how much we can get out of it. It teaches that each of your conversations unfold in a way that's unique to your history and that of the person you are speaking with.'[3]

Understanding is about developing the discipline of focusing on, and achieving clarity about, what the other person is saying as the *initial* goal in any conversation. **Challenging** explores how to test what's being said in a way that opens things up and leads to greater clarity and connection, rather than shutting things down or causing an argument. And **Being Understood** is about ensuring that what we ourselves 'transmit' is received with clarity and understanding by whoever we're talking to. Let's look at each in turn.

Chapter 3

Understanding

It's often thought that good communication basically depends on the skills of the person who's telling others what they think – the 'transmitter'. And to support this idea the world is full of books, websites and courses with titles like *How To Get Your Point Across Successfully* and *Top Tips For Effective Communicators.*

The reality is the complete opposite. The most powerful person in any conversation is actually the *listener* – the 'receiver'.

If you find this hard to believe, try a little experiment. In your next conversation, start by paying close attention to the other person as they speak. Make eye contact, nod, show real interest – and then become distracted; subtly at first but then more and more obviously. Break eye contact, look around, glance at your watch, maybe even check your phone. At some point the other person will stop talking, will ask what's wrong, if they're boring you; they might even get quite offended (so it's probably best to try this with someone you know well, as you can explain what you've been doing).

The fact is, unless we're totally self-absorbed, it's very hard to talk to someone if we don't think they're listening. We feel demotivated, disrespected even, especially if what we're trying to say is important to us. This means that in any conversation it's the listener who has the real control, who determines the outcome. To put it another way, it's in the listener's hands to *empower* the talker; first, simply by completing the process of transmission and reception – 'from your mouth to my ear' – and second, crucially, by focusing explicitly on *striving to understand* what's being transmitted.

The importance of this is hard to overstate, not least because we can listen and understand in very different ways and at very different levels.

For example, Marshall Rosenberg, the founder of nonviolent communication, famously used the image of 'jackal ears' and 'giraffe ears' to explain different ways of listening. Our jackal ears listen to find weakness and attack, to criticise and pass judgment on the speaker and what they're saying. Our giraffe ears do the opposite – they listen to empathise and understand, and are so called by Rosenberg because for him the giraffe is a symbol of compassion, being the land animal with the largest heart.

However, as trained mediators know, even listening to understand can be done in different ways. That's why they often use a model called PIN analysis to get to the core of what's really bothering people in a dispute. PIN stands for Position, Interests, Needs and can be shown as an iceberg (Figure 3.1).

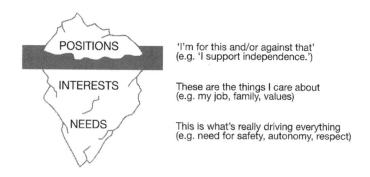

Figure 3.1 PIN analysis

Conflicts often get stuck because the opposing parties are arguing about *positions* that can't be reconciled – it's either 'this' or 'that', a zero-sum game where one side wins and the other side loses, so both sides refuse to budge. Mediators have found that by digging down into what the parties care about and what's really driving everything – their *interests* and *needs* – everyone can start to explore other ways in which these interests and needs might be met; positions can then become more flexible and might eventually change.

This model is also very useful in creative conversation. For example, we can listen to understand facts and opinions, which relates to Position. We can listen to understand emotions and values, which relates to Interests. And we can listen to understand needs, which relates to, well, Needs. Ideally, we'll be listening to understand on all three levels at once (although this is a skill that might take some time to develop). But even focusing on clarifying just facts and opinions – the most obvious part of the 'iceberg' – can have a powerful effect 'below the waterline', as Jan discovered on a trip to Peru as the guest of an international aid charity.

During my visit, I was taken to a conflict resolution initiative in a remote town in the foothills of the Andes. Earlier that year, local peasant farmers had besieged the allegedly corrupt mayor in the town hall and at midnight had dragged him out into the main square to put him through a terrifying mock execution.

I was concerned to learn more about this event and see what difference the conflict resolution process had made – but when I arrived with my translator I realised with alarm that wires had got badly crossed somewhere. The replacement mayor and his deputies had locked themselves into his office, a delegation of angry peasant farmers were camped outside his door – and they were all expecting me to actually mediate the conflict, there and then. I'd only ever had a few days training in conflict resolution, the visit was planned for just a couple of hours and tempers were still running hot. What could I do?

I asked the new mayor if everyone might sit together to talk but he shook his head – there'd be a fight. So I decided simply to listen to each group separately, without judgment; to ask them to explain from their perspective what had happened and why, and to offer what they thought might be solutions for the future.

I started with the new mayor and his deputies, who wanted those responsible for the mock execution to be locked up. A mayor at a nearby town had actually been lynched not long before on the basis of a false accusation of corruption, and the besieged mayor had genuinely feared he'd be killed.

When their turn came the farmers jostled with the mayor and deputies in the doorway – there was raw hostility on both sides. And then there was a lot of crying and angry shouting as the farmers complained about how government money for the town had been stolen – they'd only wanted to scare the mayor so the money would be spent honestly on things the town needed, like road repairs and basic sanitation. It took well over an hour for them to relay just the basic facts – by which time I had to go.

I explained that all I could do was pass on to the aid charity what both sides had said – I couldn't promise anything more. But the farmers hugged me, shook my hand, wept. And as I was leaving, to my surprise I saw the two groups start to talk to each other without trading blows.

I never found out what happened because the aid charity didn't keep in touch. But by feeling safe to vent their feelings to me, and because I'd sincerely tried to understand them, I *believe both sides were in a better position to at least begin a process of dialogue.*

As Jan discovered, creative conversation starts with us consciously taking the powerful role not just of listener, but of *understander*. By striving first to understand, we're looking to create a connection with the other person, an action to which they nearly always respond positively. And by first having connected to and understood the other person, we can then ground our own response on the clarity we've gained, calmly and considerately.

Despite the cultural differences and initially feeling completely at sea, Jan managed to connect by striving to understand the facts of the situation and the opinions – the positions – of everyone involved. If we seek to understand the emotions and needs of the speaker the results can sometimes be even more dramatic.

A woman in one of our creative conversation workshops suddenly burst into tears at the end of one of the exercises and rushed out of the room to recover.

The task had been to pair up with someone you don't know, find something you disagree about, then spend five minutes each explaining your views on the subject to the other person. During that time, the 'understander' mustn't disagree or criticise in any way. Their sole task is to demonstrate their understanding of what they're hearing. Having done that, they qualify to have their say and the roles are reversed.

The subject of this particular conversation had been whether it's better to have wooden floors or carpets in a living-room. Hardly something to get tearful about, you'd think. But when the woman returned, she apologised for breaking down and explained why.

'I've been married for seventeen years,' she said, 'and I realised my husband has never listened to me with the respect and attention shown to me by this complete stranger.'

In other words, her needs for respect and attention were not being met in her marriage – and to what cost?

'First understand' saves time, effort – and relationships. And it's not just a 'lightbulb' moment of clarity we're seeking – 'Ah, *now* I understand!' *It's a role we consciously decide to adopt and stick with until understanding is achieved.* It's a disciplined process that requires both speaking and listening dedicated to the task of achieving clarity about what the other person is saying. Unless at least one person in a conversation is consciously dedicated to that task, it's likely that full understanding won't be achieved, regardless of how much effort each person puts into trying to explain something. In fact, if the talking revolution lives anywhere, it's here, in the listener's decision to stick at 'first understand'.

Understanding doesn't mean agreeing, of course, but by first staying in the role of understander we achieve something far more valuable than simply telling someone else what we think. We give them the gift of being heard; we demonstrate respect and consideration for them; we gain a full understanding of the way they see things; and we create the conditions in which, when we do express our view, we are far more likely to be understood in return. By adopting the practice of 'first understand' we establish the basis for a real meeting of minds, through which the responsible, open, creative act of thinking together can produce new sparks of insight that neither party could have come up with individually. Understanding first can bring out the best in all of us.

Seek first to understand, then to be understood.
Steven Covey

This disciplined process of 'first understand' is made up of *four key components*, each of which is beneficial in its own right and all of which combine to lay the foundation for creative conversation – anywhere, at any time, with anyone. None of the components is revolutionary. They're just a collection of key things we humans do when we're at our best in striving to understand each other. What is revolutionary, though, is the difference these four practical, doable components make when they're applied consistently in everyday conversations.

FOCUS

The first component – **focus on whoever is speaking** – is, for obvious reasons, the most basic of all. If we don't focus on the other person, we create very little other than offence and simply sow the seeds for misunderstanding. If we do focus our attention, we not only show respect but start to forge a connection.

Ask any class of students how many times in their educational lives they've been asked to pay attention and a sea of eyes starts to roll. Ask those same students how many *lessons* they've had in 'paying attention', however, and the answer is usually a big fat zero. They're all meant to just know intuitively how to perform this essential requirement for learning. But in our 24/7-connected world, focusing on anything seems to be growing increasingly difficult. More and more things compete for our attention and multi-tasking can often seem like the only viable solution – writing an email while simultaneously talking to someone and checking out Facebook. Unfortunately, though, the benefits of multi-tasking come at a cost.

For example, have you ever been in a cafe with a friend and overheard a fascinating conversation at the next table? Your friend is talking and you're trying to listen, but this intriguing exchange right next to you keeps vying for your attention. And strangely, when your focus is fully on your friend, the 'volume' of the conversation at the next table goes down, but when you switch attention to the fascinating strangers, even momentarily, your friend's volume goes down and theirs goes up. Why?

It's because despite being equipped by evolution with a complex system of internal multi-tasking abilities – we can see, hear, smell, feel, breathe, pump blood, digest food, walk down the street and think about difficult problems all at the same time – human beings can't process two 'thinking tasks' at the same time at zero cost. We can walk and talk with someone, no problem, or do the washing-up and listen to a radio discussion; but we can't talk to someone while listening to that discussion without compromising one or the other task. Just as in the café, the volume levels go up and down as we switch our focus. Something has to give.

Moreover, while external distractions are fairly easy to identify and deal with, internal distractions are trickier. It's so natural to be so absorbed by our own thoughts that often we simply don't hear what the other person is saying. Or we may technically be 'paying attention', looking at the other person and not speaking, while actually failing to take in anything they're saying – maybe because we've inadvertently wandered off on a mental tangent and are quickly trying to recover without them noticing; or maybe we're thinking instead about what we're going to say in reply and are waiting for them to shut up so that we can deliver our pearl of wisdom.

This type of 'listening to respond' isn't really paying attention at all. It certainly isn't understanding. That's because, as with the strangers in the café, by focusing on our own thoughts we inadvertently tune out the other person and miss the opportunity to gain from whatever they're saying. It's not that what we're thinking isn't worthwhile. It's just that the most constructive point in the conversation to think and say it is *after* we've understood.

Listening to criticise, listening to judge, feeling we have to come up with something clever to say – all these things erect barriers to what could otherwise be a valuable exchange for both parties. That's why paying attention is the first step in understanding, which is the first step in creative conversation, which is the key to our own personal talking revolution.

So to start the revolution, let's turn off the radio, tear our eyes away from the screen, the phone or other people, and focus completely on the most important person in our world right now – the one in front of us. This simple act alone can make a huge a difference to our relationships with other people.

A few days after attending a workshop on creative conversation skills, primary school teacher Karen reported a conversation she'd had with nine-year-old Aakil.

Aakil: Miss – what are you doing? You're different.

Karen: I don't know what you mean.

Aakil: Yes you do. You're different, miss. What are you doing?

Karen: OK, I admit it. I'm listening to you.

'I've definitely become much better at paying attention,' explained Karen, 'and that's helped me to listen better, which has helped the children to talk more freely. There have been issues where I've now been able to get to the root of what the problem is, rather than what I'd assumed it was, and so have taken the right action to help. It just saves so much time!'

Conversations are a two-way street, so any positive changes we make in our role as an understander – or while challenging or being understood – will definitely be felt by the other person and therefore start to improve the relationship.

STAY OPEN

The second component of the disciplined process of 'first understand' is to **stay open**. This is the practical application of the principle of openness, which recognises two of our basic human tendencies when we communicate – to make assumptions and to close up if we hear something we don't like. But it's in this effort – this fight, even – to put aside our assumptions, open up and stay open to different people and different ideas, even when we strongly disagree, that the possibility of creating something of value can be born.

We've already explored our natural human tendency to close up or attack when we feel that something we care about is being threatened or denied. But as long as we're increasingly aware of our own needs, values and reactions we can *consciously choose to ignore them at that moment*, even when we're suddenly 'ambushed by anger' or some other powerful emotion. Instead, we can *choose* to focus on the person who's talking and strive to understand them. This can be difficult, of course, especially if we're also anxious that perhaps we won't get the chance to challenge or have our say. But again, the benefit of adopting this approach is to create a connection with that person through which our response, when it comes, will more likely be heard and understood in return. This is particularly effective in ongoing relationships where everything doesn't have to be achieved in a single conversation.

But there are other less obvious ways in which we tend not to be open, making assumptions being one of them.

> **Differences challenge assumptions.**
> *Anne Wilson Schaef* [1]

It's sometimes said that 'assumptions form the boundaries of our wisdom'. Or to put it another way, when we're asked to 'think outside the box' it's our assumptions that draw the sides.

It's like the old story of the policeman out on night patrol who comes across a drunk crawling around on his knees under a streetlight.

'I'm looking for my car keys,' explains the drunk.

The policeman scans the area under the streetlight. 'They're not here,' he says.

'No, I dropped them over there,' says the drunk, pointing down the road.

'So why are you looking here?' asks the policeman.

''Cos this is where the light is,' says the drunk.

Putting our assumptions on hold when we adopt the understander role means consciously choosing to step away from the 'streetlight' and out into the 'dark', because that's where we're more likely to find the 'keys'. But thinking outside the box is easier said than done. Take this box, for example (Figure 3.2). Can you join all the dots using only four straight lines, without your pen leaving the paper? (See Appendix B for the answer.)

Figure 3.2 Thinking outside the box

As with the solution here, our assumptions are often obvious only in hindsight. But being prepared to acknowledge them, to have them challenged and if necessary to discard them, is all part of staying open.

Another subtle barrier to staying open in a conversation is when we feel unqualified to take part. We tell ourselves that 'I don't really know enough about this, so I'd better keep my mouth shut.' But a true talking revolutionary will have none of that, because there are three words we can use to gain full entry to any conversation, however daunting the subject might seem. Ironically, those words are 'I don't understand.'

With this one little phrase, we set ourselves free – free to engage and free to learn. We're up and over the barricades of our ignorance and on the way to building stronger relationships, simply by consistently adopting the practice of 'first understand'.

Ali was panicking on her way to a meeting of a government consultation group. As the head of a large and successful organisation dedicated to helping troubled teenagers, she was overloaded with work and hadn't had time to read the preparation notes sent round to all the delegates. It was too late for that now – but as she pulled into the car park she had a brainwave.

'I know,' she thought, 'I'll be a good understander.'

Ali later described what happened. 'I sat down at this large board table, with all these important people, and whenever anyone said anything that wasn't clear to me – which obviously happened quite a bit – I asked would they mind clarifying it? And then I'd say something back to check I'd got it right.

'I did this for the whole meeting and when we finished a number of people sincerely thanked me for my great contribution! I knew very little when I arrived and if I hadn't

done the "understander" thing I'd have known very little when
I left as well.'

Ali turned her ignorance into something of value by first asking for an explanation, then confirming her grasp of what she was hearing by briefly summarising it. By creating these individual moments of clarity she not only gained more understanding herself, she also contributed to the understanding of the group as a whole. Which is often the way, as it's rarely one person alone who'll be struggling to make sense of something that's difficult or full of complex detail. So admitting that we don't understand can actually be a great strength – the courage to be vulnerable – and a powerful way to create new connections. But to do this we need to fight to stay open at those moments when it's easier to shut down – or simply shut up.

CLARIFY

By lowering as many external and internal barriers as we can, including the barrier of not wanting to confess our ignorance, we're effectively stretching out a 'blank canvas' in our heads on which to paint a picture of what the other person is expressing. So the third component of 'first understand' is to **clarify** our understanding of what that picture is. And the most important thing to remember here is that *it's their picture we're trying to paint*, not our interpretation of it. It's about them, not us. Imagine this scene.

Rani gets home from a long day's work at the local council. Steph, her partner, is in the kitchen making dinner, when she hears the front door close.

'Hi Rani. You OK?'

'*Yeah – what a day!*' *Rani calls back wearily from the hallway.*

'*Well, I know I'm like a cracked record,*' *says Steph as Rani comes into the kitchen,* '*but you got to get out of there, hun. They're running you into the ground.*' *She gives her a hug.* '*Glass of wine?*'

'*Er, no thanks. I think I'll have a bath.*'

Steph obviously cares about Rani. She's making a meal, offers her a drink, is concerned she's being overworked – so what's wrong here? Well, the conversation could have gone very differently.

'*Hi Rani. You OK?*'

'*Yeah – what a day!*' *Rani calls back wearily from the hallway.*

'*You sound exhausted,*' *says Steph as Rani comes into the kitchen. She gives her a hug.*

'*Knackered,*' *Rani smiles.* '*100 kids from four different schools touring the town hall. Boy, have they got some energy.*'

'*Glass of wine?*'

'*You betcher. It was great – in the end – but these school trips always seem to take everyone by surprise.*'

'*You'd like more warning?*'

'*Not just warning – planning, organisation! I mean, they happen every few months and I'm expected to drop everything and take charge at the last minute – by myself.*'

Steph hands Rani the wine. 'So you could do with some help, too.'

'Ha! That would be nice.' Rani laughs. 'Cheers.'

In the first version of the conversation, Rani arrives home from work exhausted and Steph, rather than seeking to understand her experience, simply voices her own opinion – 'You've got to get out of there, hun.' In fact, Rani's had a good day, if a tiring one, and she actually enjoys her job; but because correcting Steph's view feels like too much effort, she just decides to go and relax in the bath. Nothing terrible has happened but perhaps the two of them have fallen into this habitual way of talking – Steph makes assumptions, Rani doesn't bother to correct her and bit by bit the bandwidth of their communication has shrunk.

The key to expanding that bandwidth is to *confirm our grasp of what we're hearing by offering brief 'nuggets of understanding' along the way* – not our opinion, our judgment or our advice, but simply what we've understood. The PIN 'iceberg' can help here. We can certainly use these 'nuggets of understanding' to confirm facts and opinions but it's often more effective to identify the feelings and needs underlying what's being expressed. If we don't do this we might get the facts right but our words of 'support', however well intended, can fall short of the mark. They might even be damaging.

The second conversation goes differently because Steph uses this 'nuggets of understanding' approach. She doesn't assume anything, just expresses how she senses Rani is feeling.

'You sound exhausted.'

If Steph's wrong in this Rani has a chance to correct her – she might be more fed up than tired, say. But in this case Steph's right and, feeling understood, Rani goes on to say more. Again,

Steph offers no opinion, just support and encouragement via a glass of wine. When Rani says 'these school trips always seem to take everyone by surprise' Steph still doesn't express a view. She just feeds back her understanding of what Rani has said.

'You'd like more warning?'

This isn't quite accurate – but it prompts Rani to go into more detail.

'Not warning – planning, organisation! I mean, they happen every few months and I'm expected to drop everything and take charge at the last minute – by myself.'

Steph's response then, importantly, identifies the need beneath the surface.

'So you could do with some help, too.'

Which Rani confirms. She feels understood and supported by Steph, and their creative conversation continues over supper as they look at how things could be better organised at Rani's office. There's a lot of detail Steph doesn't know but her open, seeking approach to understanding what her partner is saying and feeling helps Rani to clarify her own thinking and see some new ways forward.

By contrast, in the first version of the conversation, Steph jumps in with her advice before understanding the issue, Rani doesn't have the energy to explain and so her needs at work are simply not uncovered. Steph feels justified in her incorrect view that Rani's in the wrong job and Rani, in turn, feels less inclined to talk to Steph about her work because she so often gets the wrong end of the stick – and tells Rani what to do into the bargain.

Steph and Rani's story is a simple, undramatic exchange between two people, where no sparks fly and no blood is spilled. But it's precisely in these small, everyday interactions that creative conversation can pay significant dividends. So many relationships, at all levels and in all areas, founder because the 'subtext' of what is being said in these exchanges – the unspoken stuff 'between the lines' – is not brought out into the open and clarified. Instead, it just sits there and gradually accumulates a life of its own, so that assumption feeds misunderstanding that reinforces assumption that eventually leads to any number of negative outcomes – rows, misjudgments, relationship failures.

Creative conversation does the exact opposite. Bit by bit it helps us build trust, expand bandwidth and solidify our one-to-one connections with each other. And by developing simple communication habits like clarifying, we can gradually build our confidence to tackle more difficult subjects – and more challenging individuals.

PROMPTS AND PROBES

In the course of clarifying something it's natural to ask questions. But strange as it might sound, this isn't always the best way to get open, clear answers. In fact, questions are like knives – they can do as much harm as good, so need to be used wisely. For example, 'What on EARTH were you thinking!!?', 'WHY haven't you done your HOMEWORK!!?' and 'WHEN are you going to SORT THIS OUT!!?' are framed as questions but they're not really attempts at clarification; they're attacks and criticisms, complaints. Even questions that aren't accusations-in-disguise can inadvertently hijack the flow of conversation in the direction of what we want to know, as opposed to what the other person is trying to say. And asking too many questions, or questions that are too direct, can make the exchange seem more like an interrogation than a conversation.

So when sticking at the role of understander, using 'prompts and probes' is an effective way to gain more clarification while avoiding the potential pitfalls of questions. Here are some examples.

TED (Tell/Explain/Describe): *Tell me a bit about what's been happening this week / Please explain the situation for me / Describe what you've been going through.*

Sharing thoughts: *I'm wondering about how that might affect X...*

Suggest and fade: *Hmm. Maybe we could come up with another way...*

Confessing confusion: *I'm really not clear about the background to all of this.*

Nudging: *Go on... Uhuh...*

Playing a hunch: *Well, it sounds to me as if...*

Self-disclosure: *You know, I was in a situation once where...*

There's also *reflecting*, which simply means repeating back a word or phrase the speaker has used to show you're listening and encourage them to continue:

'And I'm really worried – because he's 93!'

'You're worried' or just *'93?'*

While *reacting* means making a direct response to what's been said to show you understand the emotion of the speaker.

'But despite all that, she got top marks!'

'Wow. What a relief.'

Of course, questions are a normal part of how we talk to each other and they're certainly not banned from creative conversation. But in seeking clarity and understanding it's generally more effective to use open questions – what, why, when, where, how, who – rather than closed questions that demand a 'yes' or 'no' reply, as open questions allow the speaker more leeway to answer as they want.

'How are you coping?' rather than *'Are you coping?'*

But again, there's no hard-and-fast rule: ultimately, it's up to the wisdom of your 'conversation manager'(see Chapter 6) to use prompts, probes and questions in the way that will create most clarity, most understanding and most value. And don't forget the power of silence. Stopping to allow space for thought and reflection can sometimes lead to profound moments of recognition and realisation. And connection.

I have striven not to laugh at human actions, not to weep at them, nor to hate them, but to understand them.
Baruch Spinoza[2]

SUMMARISE

The fourth component of the disciplined process of under-standing is to **summarise.** We need to pull the strands together of what's been said so we can check that the 'picture' we've painted on the blank canvas of our understanding is the same picture that's in the mind of the person who's been speaking. Summarising confirms that the message sent and the message received are one and the same, so that if either the speaker or understander went off and individually recounted the conversation to another person, they'd both tell essentially the same story. There are various short phrases we can use to trigger this summary.

So what you're saying is ...

Let me see if I've got this right ...

So just to recap...

Or we can simply summarise without the preamble.

So your boss is a pig, you're totally fed up and you need to move on.

As with the 'nuggets of understanding', summarising shows the speaker that we've 'got it'. And if we haven't, it allows them to correct us – or themselves, because often the summary shows the speaker that they've not been entirely clear or said everything that's on their mind.

Another benefit of summarising is that once a chunk of the story or explanation has been confirmed as understood by both sides, the transmitter and receiver, it can act as a kind of marker-post in the conversation and the foundation for further understanding.

OK, so it's pretty clear you're unhappy and you want to change jobs. What are you thinking might be possible?

Summarising therefore needn't wait till the very end of the speaker's oration. It can come at periodic intervals, especially during long and complex conversations, to break the process of clarifying and understanding into digestible portions. These might then be rolled into a short 'summary of summaries' at the end – once again, your 'conversation manager' will take charge.

* * *

The four components might seem a bit laborious or formulaic at first, but the time and effort they save in having to deal with misunderstanding pays for the labour many times over. By employing them we lay the foundation for a creative conversation, which is built on striving to understand the other person and then demonstrating to their satisfaction that we have – before we take things further.

So just to recap ...

1. The real power in any conversation lies with the listener – and even more with the *understander*. This is why it's so important that we practise 'understanding first' and stick with this role till we properly understand what's being said.
2. PIN analysis suggests that we can listen and understand at three levels – facts and opinions (Position); emotions and things the speaker cares about (Interests); and their underlying basic needs (Needs); ideally all three. But identifying and acknowledging emotions and needs can create a stronger connection with people than simply clarifying facts and opinions.
3. 'First understand' has four practical, doable components:
   a. *Focus* – pay attention to whoever is speaking by ignoring external and internal distractions
   b. *Stay open* – consciously decide *not* to close down or counterattack on hearing unpleasant views or criticisms, watch out for assumptions and remember to use the

power of 'I don't understand' to turn ignorance into an opportunity to learn and connect

c. *Clarify* – by feeding 'nuggets of understanding' back to the speaker, using prompts and probes (and open questions, judiciously) to help them paint a clear and full picture

d. *Summarise* – by pulling together the main strands of what's been said to confirm your understanding to that point, which can then be used as the basis for further conversation.

Which all sounds pretty straightforward. But what do we do if we apply these skills and, rather than basking in the harmony of mutual understanding, we discover that we disagree with the speaker, maybe even profoundly?

This, potentially, is where the gold can be found, as the next chapter explains.

Chapter 4

Challenging

Challenging can make or break a creative conversation. Without challenge, what passes between you can be just so much talk. You might have satisfied the other person's need to be understood but when things need to be re-evaluated or myths exploded, there's nothing better than a healthy dose of upfront challenging to blow the dust off a situation and get it moving in a positive direction. Done well, challenging can open up unexplored perspectives, create valuable new insights and lead to a stronger connection between those involved. But done poorly, it can trigger defensiveness, shut things down and even end the relationship. In short, challenging can be challenging.

How, then, do we decide what to challenge and what not to, and what's the best way to go about it? This is another point where the Three Principles of creative conversation come into play, prompting us to take responsibility for keeping the exchange open and working towards creating 'something of value'.

USING NEEDS AND VALUES

Here again it's important to remember that we create value through meeting the needs of all those involved in creative conversation, including ourselves, so it can be helpful to think of challenging in these terms. Often, challenging can amount to little more than trying to assert our needs and values over someone else's, while they're trying to do the same thing to us. And often, because we or they – or both of us – are not entirely clear about which of our needs and values are at play in the conversation, the exchange gets stuck in confused debate/ argument mode. We get caught in a mishmash of opinion, emotion, disputed facts, contorted logic, blind-alley arguments and negative judgments of each other (spoken or unspoken). Each of us is trying to win rather than create 'something of value' and so we become increasingly rigid in our positions, as conceding any point means to risk 'losing'. Small wonder, then, that in this type of exchange we often end up feeling frustrated and dissatisfied – or worse.

By contrast, challenging based on the conscious attempt to meet needs and to identify, acknowledge and respect values – ours and theirs – is much more likely to produce the positive, mutually enriching result that is at the heart of creative conversation; and that's even if at the end of the process no one's opinion has shifted a jot. So here are some common challenges based on needs and values. For example, we can challenge for:

Clarity/understanding
   'Sorry, I'm not clear. Could you perhaps say a bit more about…'

Consistency
   'OK. Only I'm wondering how that squares with what you said about…'

Accuracy/honesty
   I remember it slightly differently. I thought she said…'

Authenticity
   'Is that the real you speaking, or are you maybe saying it because…'

Fairness/compassion
  'Well, what you're saying sounds fine for this group of people but let's think how that other group might respond.'

Logic/coherence/effectiveness
  'OK, I'll play devil's advocate. What happens if...?'

Order/harmony/community
  'Maybe... but might we be causing a lot of upheaval for no guaranteed benefit?'

Creativity/growth/hope
  'Yes, that's one possibility. Let's get a few more on the table...'

These are challenges based on the needs and values of the challenger but they can also serve the needs and values of the person being challenged. In seeking clarity for ourselves, for example, we can also offer that clarity to the other person.

  'You said you didn't speak out because you liked the fact that everyone seemed to be getting along with each other – for once. But I sense that maybe you also lack confidence in your opinion and didn't think it worth saying?'

  'Hmm. Maybe...'

So bearing in mind how useful it can be to anchor our challenges in an awareness of needs and values, what else can we do to maximise our ability to create 'something of value' when challenging?

UNDERSTAND FIRST

First, it's important to recognise that we need to *earn the right* to challenge. If we haven't paid attention to the other person, kept ourselves open while listening to them and demonstrated to their satisfaction that we truly do understand what they're saying, on what basis are we challenging them? That would be like saying 'I can't be bothered to understand what you think, but what I think is better anyway, so just listen to me.' Once again, then, it's crucial to understand first.

But let's say we've done all the right understanding things, the other person has confirmed that we really do get where they're coming from and... well, we think that what they're saying just doesn't stack up. There's something wrong somewhere. Maybe they're speaking like *this* but behaving like *that*. Or selling themselves (or someone else) short somehow. Or there's a gap in their thinking they just can't see. So we need to challenge – but we need to do it in a way that creates rather than destroys. That's why achieving the right mix of empathy and challenge in a creative conversation is so important and, when we get it right, so powerful.

> **Empathy without challenge is anaemic.**
> **Challenge without empathy is caustic.**
> *Gerard Egan*

So how exactly do we hit that empathy-challenge sweet spot, especially during the dynamic ebb and flow of a conversation? A famous ditty by Rudyard Kipling can help.

> I keep six honest serving-men
> (They taught me all I knew);
> Their names are What and Why and When
> And How and Where and Who.

That is, by asking What, Why, When, How, Where and Who to challenge (though not necessarily in that order) we can maximise our chances of keeping the conversation on a positive track.

Where and **When** to challenge are basically questions about context and situation, which are explored in answer to various specific questions in Chapter 6.[1] And **Who** can be challenged is answered very easily – anyone with whom we're holding a creative conversation. If we're observing the Three Principles and Three Practices a challenge is unlikely to cause offence or transgress some kind of status boundary – just the opposite – provided the **Why**, **What** and **How** are consistent with the spirit of creative conversation. So let's focus on those three.

WHY CHALLENGE?

The answer to this lies in the word 'challenge' itself. Unlike 'disagreement', 'confrontation' or 'criticism', 'challenge' implies a test that might prove or disprove a thing's worth, or even lead to something better. The challenges we take on in life are crucial to our learning and development, for example, and challenging in the context of creative conversation is no different – it holds up what's being said for healthy examination and, ideally, for further advance. Perspective requires more than one point of view and challenge introduces the element of dissonance, of difference, which is essential to our growth and survival. Monocultures tend to be less resilient to environmental stress than biodiverse cultures, and human groups similarly have greater resilience when the differences they embrace are acknowledged – even encouraged – and put to good use.

In the context of creative conversation, challenging helps us see and use difference constructively. Using challenge in this positive manner to explore different views has long existed in negotiation and counselling psychology. It is also increasingly being adopted by security agencies to transform confrontational 'interrogations' into exploratory 'interviews', simply because they've proved to be more effective in prompting the interview subjects to talk freely.

For many people, though, the challenge implicit in voicing differing views can feel uncomfortable and so is often best avoided. Statements like 'I didn't want to hurt their feelings' or 'I don't want to cause a row' can be proxies for 'I didn't want to have my own feelings hurt' or 'I want to say something but I'm not sure how to handle it'.

So at this point it's important to ask – how do *you* feel personally about challenging? If someone says or does something that you think could benefit from being seen differently, are you more likely to speak up or keep quiet? And how do you tend to feel when you yourself are challenged? In other words, what's your default position? How useful has your usual approach to challenging been in talking about the things that matter to you? And why might you have developed it?

Some people are very comfortable with challenging and being challenged; they love debate and get a buzz from argument and confrontation. Others hate it, to the extent that they'll let things pass that really ought to be questioned or back down when questioned themselves. But in a creative conversation both approaches can be problematic. The debate approach tends to push the exchange towards argument, deadlock and polarisation, as discussed earlier; while the 'anything for a quiet life' approach risks thoughts and feelings never being expressed, let alone taken into account and acted on.

There are many reasons why we don't challenge and fear often plays a central role – fear of the other person's reaction, fear of confrontation or humiliation or of not being liked. A bit of laziness and complacency can get in there too – when we decide to just put up with a problem or wait for someone else to solve it for us. Then there's lack of knowledge – we sense something's not quite right but hold back from speaking up because we haven't got the facts to hand, or perhaps simply haven't had a chance to order our thoughts. But all of these feelings risk wasting a good problem, which the alchemy of creative conversation could transform into valuable progress.

What's more, every time we allow these kinds of feelings to dominate makes it more likely that we'll hold back again next time the need to challenge arises – and thus a habit of not challenging, of staying silent when something important needs saying, is born. Such habits can grow very quickly, like weeds in a garden, and before we know it a whole range of unhelpful or unhappy situations can take root in different areas of our lives because we don't have the confidence, or maybe the simple know-how, to challenge them.

Ironically, those very same feelings of discomfort can become critical tools that help us prevent conversations from ploughing their old familiar rut (or forever being side-stepped), and turn them into creative exchanges that actually bring about greater understanding, deeper connection and even practical change.

The moment of deciding whether or not to speak up is a bit like being the passenger in a car when you think the driver might have taken a wrong turn. Do you remain silent and wait to see if you're correct? Or do you take a little leap of courage and say 'I'm not sure we're going the right way'? That moment might feel a bit uncomfortable – you're uncertain and your statement could be taken as a criticism – but any self-respecting talking revolutionary would rather speak up to stay on track, than stay silent and keep going down what might be the wrong road. So it's actually that feeling of discomfort that provides the signal to act.

These seemingly small decisions are very important. By choosing *not* to challenge – to avoid discomfort – unsatisfactory situations can keep going round in the same old circles, small errors can become big ones and everyone can lose out.

All of this means that the spirit with which we challenge is crucial. A challenge made with a constructive spirit is like the grit in an oyster that produces a beautiful pearl, whereas a challenge made with a destructive spirit is like grit in an unwashed salad – it ruins the whole meal.

Mo had a problem. She ran a busy hair salon – six people crammed into a modest space in the centre of town – and Craig was probably the most talented stylist of them all. But his bad moods were toxic, creating an atmosphere that made it difficult to breathe – not for the clients, but his colleagues. At the start of the week a new apprentice, Leah, had forgotten to book in an appointment for an important client but Craig's angry reaction was way over the top – and three days later he still wasn't speaking to her.

Mo knew she had to talk to him. They'd been colleagues a long time but before now she'd let it go – she didn't relish the thought of confronting him and the moods always passed. But Leah was talking about leaving – she'd quit her last job because personal issues like this were never addressed – and Mo definitely didn't want to go through the hassle of finding someone new.

She decided to act. She got what she wanted to say to Craig clear in her head, arranged a time at the end of business on Saturday when they wouldn't be interrupted, then took a deep breath and began.

'Craig. Thanks for waiting. I want to have a chat about how things are here in the salon, especially with you and Leah.'

Craig's smile disappeared. He tensed. Mo continued.

'This is a great team and everyone's important to its success – especially you, Craig. So, I'm wondering what we can learn from what's happened over the last few days – so we can all get on better together.'

Craig went straight into attack mode. 'Well, what I've learned is that when the new girl ruins a relationship with a regular client it's Muggins here who has to sort it out – on top of everything else he's got to do.'

Mo frowned. 'You thought that relationship was "ruined" – as in over?'

Craig backtracked slightly. 'Well, not exactly – but it had to be sorted. By me!'

Mo kept her cool. 'Yes, and you handled it well, as I said at the time – with thanks. But that's not the main issue. It's the moods, the atmospheres that follow.' Craig opened his mouth to shoot back a response, then closed it and stared at the floor. 'I value you, Craig,' said Mo. 'And I also value Leah and everyone else – the whole team. So we need to find a way where when we make a mistake you don't blow a gasket, or just shut off from everyone.'

Craig was silent. Then he sighed heavily.

'Yeh. Well… It's… Thing is, I just get into this… fug, this… anger. And I don't know how to get out of it – till it just… goes.'

'Well, shall we talk about it then?' said Mo. 'What we can do, what you can do, that might help?'

Craig thought for a moment. 'OK,' he said. And so they talked.

Our approach to conflict or rudeness and disrespect can lead in many directions – and all too often those directions are negative. Like Leah in her previous job, we often 'deal with' unpleasant situations by learning to live with them or just walking away. But Leah found herself back in a similar situation, while her former employer's failure to challenge problems had led to low morale and the loss of at least one employee. Mo, too, had previously not challenged Craig about his behaviour, even though a positive outcome was actually there for the taking. In fact, after the weekend Craig apologised to everyone, specifically to Leah, and made a promise to change the angry side of his behaviour. He thanked them all for putting up with him – and suddenly everyone was on his side, impressed by his honesty and willing to support him.

So by adopting a responsible, open-minded and creative approach – the Three Principles in action – Mo helped Craig, and therefore her whole business, achieve a positive, mutually beneficial outcome. With the added bonus that she also acknowledged and was able to overcome her own blindspot about failing to challenge.

To sum up, the **Why** question goes to the very purpose of creative conversation, which – and it bears repeating – is *to create 'something of value' by seeking to meet the basic human needs of everyone involved.* The most fundamental of these include the need for connection, respect and understanding. It stands to reason, then, that a challenge made within a creative conversation must, at a minimum, not deny these needs; that is, it must not disrespect, deliberately misunderstand or wilfully break the connection with the other person. Which can be pretty challenging itself if we hear something we really don't like. But it is possible – with practice. Which brings us to **What** and **How.**

WHAT TO CHALLENGE

The rule of thumb here is 'Challenge the person's thoughts, words or deeds – not the person.' As with so many aspects of creative conversation, though, this can be easier said than done. The BBC journalist John Simpson famously said of Nelson Mandela, 'He always spoke to the great person he knew you could be' and that's a good guideline for the spirit of challenging;

it helps us to focus on the fundamental dignity of the other person and their right to hold their view. And respecting the person, while challenging what they think, say or do, actually creates a stronger platform from which to hold up any aspect of their thoughts, words or behaviour for examination. This isn't easy, of course, but the PIN model we explored in the previous chapter can help to clarify the process.

For example, while respecting that everyone has a right to their way of seeing the world, we can still challenge the facts and opinions (Position) that a person is expressing – 'You say he's impossible to work with, but what you've described doesn't seem unreasonable to me. Perhaps he's struggling too?'

We can also challenge what they care about (Interests) and their emotions, to help them gain a (new) sense of perspective. Sometimes people care too much – 'I can see you're very angry but I'm wondering if that's actually going to get you the result you want?' And sometimes they don't care enough – 'If you don't start looking after your health, well, you could do yourself some real damage.' We can even challenge a person's perception of their needs – 'You keep saying you need help, Mum, but do you think maybe what you're really looking for is company?' As always in creative conversation, the challenge seeks to open up space or reframe the current situation so that new possibilities might be explored.

That said, let's look more closely at three common examples of **what** can be challenged to bring about the positive outcomes that creative conversation strives to achieve.

1. Limiting attitudes or beliefs

Many of us can be our own worst enemy. How often do we think of ourselves – and/or others – as being incapable of things that could in fact be achieved? And how often do we believe things that limit us or others in some way – that 'such-and-such is not for the likes of me (or you)'? Thinking like this is actually very common – universal, even – and can quietly, unconsciously, come to dictate the direction of our lives, to the point that we might never fulfil our true potential. We need to challenge and be challenged – as family members, friends and colleagues – to make sure that our thinking, and the thinking of those around us, remains open and alive to possibility. So challenging isn't only about pointing to what might be wrong – it is also about helping to reveal undiscovered, ignored or even forgotten positives.

This is such a fundamental aspect of human life that stories about it are told just about everywhere, in just about every culture and just about every period. Typically, something forces the hero/heroine to meet a series of tests, each one more difficult than the last, and to find and develop from within themselves the strength, skills and ingenuity to overcome the challenges and win the ultimate prize – freedom, success, fulfilment, love – whatever it might be. But at some point (in all the best stories, anyway), a key challenge will be the hero/heroine's lack of belief in their own abilities, maybe even their own worth. They will consider giving up on the task, giving up on themselves, or even giving up on everything – think of Hamlet's 'To be or not to be' speech, possibly the most famous in all of world literature. At this crucial moment – or moments, as the hero/heroine might be plagued with self-doubt throughout the story – they will either find some hidden strength or, often, another character in the story will somehow challenge their negativity and encourage their fighting spirit (challenge and encouragement nearly always go hand-in-hand). This basic narrative pattern appears again and again, from the oldest story that humanity knows – *The Epic of Gilgamesh* – to what we hear and read daily in the news media; and, indeed, in what we actually experience in our everyday lives and struggles.

Jenna wanted to run her own restaurant but was stuck working as a lowly commis chef in a series of hotel kitchens.

Then she heard about a chance to train for three weeks with one of the world's top chefs in New York. She wrote a heartfelt letter to the chef – and was stunned to be accepted. But the offer wasn't free – there were flights, accommodation, living expenses – and Jenna simply didn't have the money. There was no way she could earn it in the time before the deadline either. Her golden opportunity seemed about to slip away...

Until a friend suggested a telesales job with an eye-watering pay structure – one sale would pay the basic commission, the second sale would pay double *the basic, three sales would pay* four *times the amount, four sales* eight *times the amount, and so on. Not that anyone had ever made more than four sales in a shift.*

Jenna was excited – here was the chance to make the money she needed in the few weeks available – and a phone call later she was hired. But she quickly discovered why the job was so well-rewarded – hardly anyone wanted to buy the product. Call after call produced nothing and after two weeks she'd made less than if she'd stayed working in a restaurant.

Disheartened, dispirited, she poured out her woes to her favourite aunt, who was like a mentor to her.

'So you've given up?'

Jenna shrugged. 'What can I do? It's impossible.'

'Hmm. So no one's ever made four sales in a shift?'

'Once – only.'

'Three sales?'

'Well, there's this one guy who seems to have the magic knack, but everyone else...' She shrugged again, this time with a sigh.

'So it is possible then. The real question is why you think it's not possible for you.'

They talked some more and when Jenna next went in to work something seemed to have changed. She closed three sales that shift, four a couple of shifts later – she was amazed – and by the time she left she was the top telesales person in the company. She got her money on time, went to New York, and went on to make a successful career as a professional chef. So what was the secret?

'My aunt said something that really made me think. She said 'If you believe this training is so important for you, for your future, you'll find a way to get the money.' That was it. But somehow, for some reason, it changed my attitude deep down. A part of me decided that failing just wasn't an option – I had to go to New York. And the weird thing was, after our talk I really didn't do anything different at work. I mean, we had a script and we had to stick to it. Maybe my tone of voice was different, or maybe I was giving off a different vibe or something – I don't know. But looking back, what I needed to learn was the importance of my basic attitude, that total determination moment to moment, because that affected everything. The New York gig was great, don't get me wrong. But the struggle to get there was the real lesson.'

Jenna's story has the typical ups and downs, breakthroughs and reverses, of a classic hero/heroine narrative, including the point of fundamental self-doubt when the goal seems impossible. And the turning-point comes when her aunt (the trusted guide/ally) *challenges* Jenna on how she sees her situation.

> *'So it is possible then. The real question is why you think it's not possible for* you.'

By creating that moment of cognitive dissonance – that element of mental discomfort, like the piece of grit in an oyster – her aunt is able to shift Jenna from looking outwards at her problem, to inwards at her own thinking. It's a shift that helps Jenna hear her aunt's simple advice – and reflect on it – at a level deep enough for Jenna to want to change her behaviour in a subtle but significant way. It was truly a creative conversation – and at its heart was a creative challenge.

2. Blindspots

Like Jenna, we can never see ourselves as others see us. However self-aware we try to be, we all inevitably have blindspots, aspects of our thinking and behaviour – positive and negative – that simply escape us. But not those around us; especially, often, our nearest and dearest. Take another example – Rani and Steph, the young couple we met earlier.

When Rani comes home from work, Steph thinks she's being caring and supportive by saying Rani's employers are running her into the ground and she should get another job; Steph is blind to her own longstanding habit of jumping in with an opinion and advice before fully grasping the facts. But Rani has a blindspot too – her tendency to put up with things or simply withdraw if her needs aren't being met. And since neither blindspot is challenged, chances are they'll both get stuck in the same behavioural circles – maybe throughout their relationship, or maybe until something breaks. Either way, their blindspots are effectively denying them the chance to grow in those areas.

> **My greatest challenge has been to change the mindset of people. Mindsets play strange tricks on us. We see things the way our minds have instructed our eyes to see.**
> *Muhammad Yunus*[2]

Challenging a blindspot is a positive, then. If a friend doesn't realise their behaviour is creating problems and we fail to point it out, how true a friend are we? This also applies if someone doesn't see their qualities and talents, or simply takes them for granted. By pointing to their blindspot we might set them on a more productive, or even completely different, path. But blindspots are often sensitive areas, so how we do this needs care and compassion.

Blindspots are not limited to individuals. Organisations of all shapes and sizes have them, as do entire societies. Culture has been described as 'the way we do things around here' – that is, how any particular group normalises and approves certain patterns of thinking and behaving, while outlawing other patterns of thinking and behaving or even making them taboo. Blindspots that hold back development – for example, by always failing to include certain people in decision-making – can thus become embedded in organisational and social culture. And at the very worst blindspots can cause immense damage, as with the historic failure to guard against child sexual abuse that is continuing to emerge in various countries, and the widespread and ongoing sexual harassment of women.

It stands to reason, then, that individuals, families, organisations and societies that make challenging central to their culture are not just less likely to develop dangerous blindspots; they're also more likely to advance and progress.

3. Interpretations of facts or events

We live in an age where it's becoming more difficult to say with any certainty – beyond our direct experience – what's real and what's invented. Online, fake news is everywhere. And fake people, too – the myriad trolls, bots and shills who 'populate' social media platforms in order to spread disinformation and amplify social division. As the US comedian Stephen Colbert has observed, 'It used to be, everyone was entitled to their own opinion but not their own facts. But that's not the case anymore. Facts matter not at all. Perception is everything.' Which means that those who can dominate the shaping of our perceptions can increasingly dominate our reality – and influence it in ways that suit their interests, rather than the interests of society as a whole.

If a culture of honesty, integrity and respect for accuracy is what we want, we can start by taking personal responsibility for creating and maintaining that culture in our own relationships, our own human networks. If we don't, our failure to challenge interpretations of facts and events that we know – or simply suspect – to be inaccurate can be taken as tacit acceptance of them. Myths (and lies) grow, become woven into the public consciousness and the accepted narrative of our times, and gradually warp public debate and decision-making. So challenging interpretations of facts and events, large or small, as Mo did in her conversation with Craig, needs to become a standard part of our daily diet of creative conversation.

Craig had asserted that the relationship with an important client had been 'ruined', but Mo's challenge caused him to qualify his description. Had she let it go, which in the short term might have felt easier, this detail could have become an accepted part of the story and the mutually beneficial outcome for the salon might not have been achieved.

Challenging the interpretation of facts can be a great stimulus for creative conversation – unless those interpretations are held by ourselves or others to be actual, incontrovertible facts in themselves, embedded in starkly opposing views of the world. At times like this, when people see things very differently, going deeper and seeking to connect, understand and challenge at the level of emotions, values and needs can be the most effective way to make progress. But this is far from easy and the more we care about the subject, the harder it gets.

Josh and his British girlfriend, Angie, were visiting his parents in Kentucky – and Josh was worried. Angie was a left-leaning, cosmopolitan urbanite, and sitting down to dinner together was the first time she'd met his gun-owning, right-leaning father, Pete. Josh expected sparks – or worse. His mum Donna put a big plate of meat in the middle of the table.

'Venison,' said Pete. 'Shot it myself.'

'Wow,' said Angie.

Josh winced. What conflicting emotions was she hiding behind that single syllable?

'They're pests round here,' said Pete. 'White-tails. Gotta keep 'em down one way or another.'

'I've... no idea how it feels to kill an animal,' said Angie evenly.

Pete studied her for a moment but couldn't see any disapproval. 'Well, it's quite a charge,' he said, 'especially when you take down a big old buck. This one's smaller though – more tender.'

Josh glanced nervously at Angie – but her reply surprised him. It sounded as if she were genuinely curious.

'So it's exciting, a buzz?'

'Yuh, it is – but it's also necessary,' said Pete, forking the meat onto his plate. 'They destroy everything. Farmland, trees, gardens. We'd have a wasteland here if they weren't hunted."

'So there's an environmental side to it?' said Angie.

'Damn right,' said Pete. 'Two for the price of one – environmental protection plus the thrill of the kill. Three – when you count putting food on the table.'

Angie looked up at the gun cabinet on the wall behind Pete.

'It's so different in the UK,' she said. 'Meat comes from the supermarket, ready-wrapped. And all this gun stuff – it's so hard for us Brits to understand. We put it together with the gun crime figures, which are way higher here than back home, or in Europe even, and – well...'

'Yuh, I know. Lots of folks see it that way,' said Pete. He sounded thoughtful. As the meal continued, he explained what it meant to him to live close to nature, and the conversation widened to explore the differences between British and American attitudes to all kinds of things.

Later that evening Josh told Angie how good it felt to have a calm conversation about anything to do with guns. 'It's so easy for that subject to get out of hand.'

'I just decided I wasn't going to argue,' said Angie. 'Just really try to understand how he saw it all.'

Josh's concerns before the meal were based on his assumption that Angie and Pete would take up their standard Positions and attack-defend-counterattack in the usual, unproductive way. But Angie decided not to play that game. Instead, she sought to understand Pete's Interests (his love of hunting and nature) and his Needs (to protect and provide, and for freedom); and realising that he didn't need to defend himself, Pete relaxed and was able to hear how Angie saw the world.

Put simply, her challenge came not through confrontation but indirectly, through highlighting the difference between UK and US cultural attitudes. Neither she nor Pete tried to change the other's views but both understood more at the end of the meal than they did at the beginning. 'Something of value' had been created for each of them – and Josh and Donna, too, because the positive effects of a creative conversation aren't limited only to those most directly involved.

Broadly speaking, then, challenges to a person's needs, values and core belief have to be handled with care – because these are the things we all most care about. They help shape our identity – our picture of ourselves – and we can be hyper-sensitive to any (perceived) attacks on them. If our needs, values or core belief change, they will most likely do so gradually, over time, and usually not without us putting up a fight – internally and externally – to defend them.

HOW TO CHALLENGE

There's no set formula for challenging well in a creative conversation – but there are plenty of all-too-familiar ways to challenge poorly. Here are a few examples;

Rejection
'You're just wrong.'

Condemnation/labelling
'That is just racist/evil/dishonest.'

Devaluing the message
'That's completely irrelevant/ridiculous.'

Devaluing the messenger
  'That's the sort of argument I'd expect from a six-year-old.'

Attacking the messenger
  'You're just too sensitive/unfeeling.'

Getting emotional
  'One more word from you and I'll get so angry...'

Setting traps
  'So what you're saying is [a]?
  'Yes...'
  'Which means [b] – right?'
  'Erm...'
  'So therefore [c] – hmm?' (aka 'Gotcha!')

Fact-bombing
  'I've heard what you think but [a fact], [b fact], [c fact] ...'

Appealing to the crowd
  'Well, you're in a minority of one if you think that!'

Appealing to the past
  'Why should I listen to you when you were wrong about that other thing?'

Turning up the volume
  'No, no, no [raises voice] No, YOU listen to ME...

Misinterpreting
  'So, basically, what you're saying is [a].'
  'No.'
  Proceeds to criticise [a]

We can all probably add to this list of poor challenges because we've all experienced them – and almost certainly made them, too. What they have in common is the dynamics of debate rather than of dialogue; the desire to win a point rather than create something new together. The difference is reflected in the history of the words themselves. 'Debate', for example, derives from the Latin word *battuere*, meaning 'to beat/fight', whereas 'dialogue' derives from the Greek *dialogos*, meaning (roughly) 'through words'; while 'converse' derives from the Latin *conversari*, which means 'to keep company with'.

So how, in a creative conversation, can we challenge based on the collaborative spirit of *dialogos* and *conversari*, rather than the combative spirit of *battuere*? Well, sometimes a mere facial expression or a silence can do it. Sometimes a statement:

'Maybe there's another way to look at it.'

Sometimes a request:

'Could you walk me through the logic of that again?'

Or sometimes the offer or suggestion of some simple facts:

'I know you said those courses aren't available any more – but I think there's a local college that might offer them.'

All of these are challenges designed to encourage the other person to think again, to re-examine or possibly modify what they're saying. But whatever the form of the challenge, there are four basic qualities that can help keep it on track during a creative conversation. They're easily remembered as TIPS – Tentative, Invitational, Positive and Specific.

Tentative, Invitational, Positive, Specific

Challenges can be most effective when they're delivered in a way that offers the other person space to explore other approaches while also preserving their dignity, rather than condemnations that paint them into a corner. Blank accusations like 'You always do this' or 'You never do that' can simply cause offence and prompt withdrawal or a counter-attack from the other person; in order to justify their own position, they'd have to prove you wrong. But more tentative phrases – like 'I'm wondering whether…' or 'It seems to me that…' – are far more likely to open up both the person and the subject, as they're easier to consider or reject without hostility. For example, Mo didn't start her conversation with Craig by cornering him.

> *'Your bad moods could lose us a valuable employee, so how are you going to shape up?'*

Instead, she framed the conversation as a joint exploration.

> *'I'm wondering what we can learn from what's happened over the last few days – so we can all get on better together.'*

The second version implies that Mo has not already made her mind up about anything – Craig deserves his input too – and that she wants to create a solution *with* him, rather than putting him on the spot or laying down the law.

Another way to challenge tentatively is to be *indirect*, like Angie was with Pete. People often equate challenge with confrontation, which can prompt a defensive or antagonistic response. An indirect challenge avoids this as it's not confrontational. There are two basic approaches. The first is to make the challenge impersonal. For example, rather than saying 'I disagree' or, worse, 'You're wrong', we can take ourselves out of the picture altogether.

'So how do you react to the view that...?' Or *'A lot of people seem to think that...'*

If that's not possible or desirable for some reason, we can simply offer an alternative view without criticising or rejecting what we've heard.

'I see things differently – and here's why.'

Our alternative might then be considered or rejected but the focus will be on the issue at hand – and ideally the emotions, values and needs that underly it – rather than a personal battle of wills. This approach is closely related to the next tip...

Tentative, **Invitational**, Positive, Specific

A suggestion is, in essence, an invitation to think (differently) about something – and it's very hard to be offended by an invitation. So rather than trying to tell someone how or what to think, creative conversation uses understanding to get all the relevant cards on the table and agreed, then uses challenging to invite the other person to consider together some different ways of looking at them. In this way, the other person can feel more ownership of the outcome, less need to defend their original position, and he or she can emerge with their dignity intact, rather than feeling hammered into submission by our 'advice' or 'superior' thinking.

Again, rather than telling Craig he had to change his behaviour 'or else', Mo invited him to consider the possibility that he could.

'Well, shall we talk about it then?' said Mo. 'What we can do, what you can do, that might help?'

Craig thought for a moment. 'OK,' he said. And so they talked.

Craig reflected briefly, then accepted Mo's invitation, and in this way they created together a nugget of mutual understanding. There can be great strength in these quietly arrived at agreements.

Angie's indirect challenge to Pete can also be seen as a form of invitation – by simply describing an alternative view she was *inviting* him to see his love of guns in a different light. She didn't insist that one view was right and the other wrong; she just effectively held them up side by side – and in doing so strengthened her connection with Pete, so the conversation could continue and deepen.

Tentative, Invitational, **Positive**, Specific

Challenges can be driven by all kinds of motives – the need to let off steam, to defend ourselves, to point out other people's faults or to take any opportunity to make our BIG POINT. But when there's a clear need to make genuine progress, or simply to make a basic connection with the other person, it's important for the tone of the whole conversation to be unmistakably positive; not in a forced way, but in a spirit of genuinely working towards a beneficial outcome. It needs to be evident from our attitude and approach that whatever challenge we make is aimed at creating value, rather than carrying any hint of concealed attack. Again, that positive quality was clear a number of times in Mo's conversation with Craig.

'This is a great team and everyone's important to its success – especially you, Craig.

'I value you, Craig,' said Mo. 'And I also value Leah and everyone else – the whole team. So we need to find a way

where when we make a mistake you don't blow a gasket, or just shut off from everyone.'

Not only does Mo twice praise Craig directly, her final comment shows that she's realistic about people making mistakes but wants to make sure that, as far as possible, the damage is limited – for everyone. In fact, positivity imbues Mo's entire approach to this problem and is ultimately what brings Craig onside. She makes it clear that she *cares* – about him and Leah and everyone else – and so gains his trust at a time when he's actually quite vulnerable. Being genuinely positive when challenging others can be an extremely powerful means of moving everyone into a more constructive, creative space.

> Everyone has a responsibility to not only tolerate another person's point of view, but also to accept it eagerly as a challenge to your own understanding. And express those challenges in terms of serving other people.
> *Arlo Guthrie*[3]

Tentative, Invitational, Positive, **Specific**

A good way to challenge without dealing a mortal blow is to be specific. 'This whole idea of you going back to school is ridiculous' not only sounds crushing but simply isn't as effective a challenge as 'I'm concerned about how much it'll cost' or 'We need to think through how it could affect the kids.' A specific challenge like this helps the other person focus on the particular issues that need to be addressed and opens up space for a creative conversation on the subject. Again, Mo was very specific about the focus of the conversation when she spoke with Craig...

'I want to have a chat about how things are here in the office, especially with you and Leah.'

'But that's not the main issue. It's the moods, the atmospheres that follow.'

'It's the relationships between us all that matter.'

She didn't criticise Craig's entire personality but isolated a specific aspect of his behaviour that had been causing trouble for everyone – including, as it turned out, for Craig himself. The response was then 'How do we address this specific thing?' rather than 'You're such a [negative quality] person and therefore…'. Being specific can make problems and issues between us much more manageable, and their solutions much more doable.

*   *   *

So be tentative and avoid painting someone into a corner. Invite others to consider other ways of seeing things, rather than enforcing your view and demanding compliance. Make your challenge a positive experience aimed at a positive outcome. And be specific so that they know it's that particular thought, word or deed that's up for examination, not their whole worth as a human being.

As with other aspects of creative conversation, building TIPS into our interactions with others might feel a bit clunky at first, but after a time they become second nature. And the irony is that by challenging in this way – by seeking to make a connection or strengthen our relationship with the other person – it's actually much more likely that we'll have an influence on them than if we expend energy in debate and argument.

WORDS MATTER

One last observation before moving on to the next chapter (although this is also highly relevant to Being Understood); namely that it helps to be aware that many of the words we use in normal speech are 'pre-loaded' with value judgments. This is another of the key insights that underpins Marshall Rosenberg's philosophy of nonviolent communication.

> One kind of life-alienating communication is the use of moralistic judgments that imply wrongness or badness on the part of people who don't act in harmony with our values. Such judgments are reflected in language such as, 'The problem with you is that you're too selfish.' 'She's lazy.' 'They're prejudiced.' 'It's inappropriate.' Blame, insults, put-downs, labels, criticism, comparison and diagnoses are all forms of judgment.[4]

Another form of alienating language that Rosenberg highlights is that which implicitly denies that we and others have personal responsibility for our thoughts, words and actions. As he notes, 'The use of the common expression "have to" as in "There are some things you have to do, whether you like it or not" illustrates how personal responsibility is obscured in such speech.' Which contradicts one of the Three Principles of creative conversation, of course.

We're all sensitive to this judgmental and directive use of language when we hear it as aimed at us but, unfortunately, tend not to be as sensitive when we use it ourselves. So it's important to become aware of the language we use and the effect it can have on others, even if we think we're speaking with a good intention. A challenge during a creative conversation, for example, is more likely to bring about a positive outcome when we use language that is non-judgmental and implies choice, rather than lack of choice or obligation.

Well, you're getting fat 'cos you sit around all day. You should get some exercise.

Well, if you're worried about your weight, how do you feel about getting more exercise?

The first example is heavy with disapproval, shaming and judgment – the listener is experiencing a bad result ('getting fat') thanks to their bad behaviour ('you sit around all day'). They're then told what to do ('You should get some exercise') in a way that implies they currently take no exercise. By contrast, the second example reflects the problem back to the listener, without judgment, in a way that echoes their feelings ('If you're worried about your weight'); and then offers a suggestion that implies they already take some exercise and could do more – the choice is theirs. Often, simply using 'could' instead of 'should' can make all the difference – 'You could do some voluntary work' sounds much more open than 'You should do some voluntary work', for example. And phrasing it as a tentative suggestion (remembering TIPS) is more open still – 'How about maybe doing some voluntary work?'

Words can also carry what might be called 'cultural judgment' that reflects power structures and assumptions in society. Often, these judgments are 'hidden in plain sight'; that is, they are so embedded in everyday language that they're simply accepted as normal – until they are pointed out. Much of the language around gender, for example, has only become visible because women have increasingly drawn attention to how it expresses an implicit assumption of 'male as superior/dominant/positive' and 'female as inferior/submissive/negative' (Table 4.1).

This aspect of language is called 'semantic derogation' – words are used to show someone or something as being of little worth – and isn't limited to gender. Language relating to class and ethnicity, to nationality, to physical and mental capacity, even to how we look, is charged with an implied negative

Table 4.1 Some examples of semantic derogation and gender

Major	military officer
Majorette	twirls a baton
Governor	person in charge
Governess	private teacher
Bachelor	unmarried, virile, desirable
Spinster	unmarried, old, unwanted
Stud	sexually athletic
Slut	promiscuous
'Men and women'	male precedes female
'Husband and wife'	male precedes female
'Sons and daughters'	male precedes female
'Brothers and sisters'	male precedes female

judgment. When it doesn't apply to us personally (or people we care about) we're often simply unaware of it – it disappears into one of those blindspots mentioned earlier. But when it comes closer to home we notice it – because it hurts. It denies our need for respect, consideration, acceptance and more.

In short, words matter. And as we become more practised in creative conversation we'll find ourselves using them more sensitively to bring about the positive outcomes we desire, even when we're challenging a difficult subject – or person.

So just to recap...

1. In creative conversation, we challenge with the spirit of trying to add extra value in some way to the exchange.

2. We earn the right to challenge by understanding first – and checking with the other person that we've understood correctly.
3. 'Empathy without challenge is anaemic. Challenge without empathy is caustic.' The aim is to find the sweet-spot, where challenge moves things forward positively.
4. Kipling's 'six honest serving-men' can help by asking What, Why, When, Where, Who and How to challenge.
5. When it comes to 'what', common areas to challenge are blindspots, limiting attitudes and beliefs, and interpretations of fact and events. Challenging other people's needs, values and core beliefs must be handled with care.
6 When it comes to 'how', TIPS are useful – that is, to be Tentative, Invitational, Positive, Specific. And remember to avoid using words pre-loaded with value judgments and criticism.

* * *

So far in discussing the Three Practices we've focused on being in a reactive role, striving to understand what the other person is saying, and challenging to clarify or deepen that understanding or to develop something new together. But what about if we want to *initiate* a conversation? How do we best ensure that what we want to say is both clear – and clearly understood?

Chapter 5

Being Understood

First, it's crucial to note that being clear and being clearly understood are not the same thing. Whenever we speak to someone, for example, they will definitely understand *something* – but is it what we want them to understand? We could say something and the listener might, for example, understand that we're not interested in having a conversation but just want to make a speech. Or that what we're saying doesn't make any sense. Or that it 'sort of' makes sense but there's an important gap – which they'll then fill by making up something that seems to fit. In other words, what they understand might not be what we intended at all. Even with something as apparently simple as when we give someone street directions, they might say they understand – and then get lost. So was that because our directions were unclear or was their understanding at fault? Or both, perhaps? Kara works in an office in central London.

'When things are really busy,' she says, 'people only use a few words to communicate and often the message doesn't come across clearly. And then the other person starts to get anxious and blame themselves for it – they're like, "I don't understand what they said…"

'My advice is just go back and get some clarity but often they're too scared, especially with the more senior people in the firm. And then they're wasting time trying to figure out

what they're supposed to do, and maybe the wrong letter goes out or something. Whereas a one-minute conversation could have sorted everything.'

As this everyday example illustrates, there can be a vast difference between telling someone something and what they actually understand by it. And the negative consequences that can flow from that difference – in terms of wasted time and money, and potentially damaged relationships – can be vast too.

Put simply, we cannot assume that how a message is transmitted and how it's received are one and the same. And although as the speaker – the transmitter – we're only one half of this equation, in a creative conversation (and remembering the Three Principles) we're actually responsible for *both* parts, transmission and reception. That is, since we speak to be understood, we're responsible both for the clarity of what we transmit *and* for ensuring that it's been received and understood by the other person. And paradoxically, this is true even when we're *not* clear about something.

If that sounds confusing, don't worry – it will all be explained in the following pages. So let's start with our side of the equation – what we transmit.

'EMPATHIC' EXPRESSION

How we express ourselves plays a huge part in what finally arrives in the mind of the other person. If we have something important to say but we state it in a way that's hard to hear – it's unclear, say, or uncaring or judgmental – the chances of it being fully understood are diminished *because the needs of the person we're speaking to aren't being met*. To put it another way, empathy doesn't operate only when we're in understand/listening mode – we're also most effective as talkers when we can hear ourselves with the ears of those listening to us.

Katie was a trainee history teacher who wanted to ignite a passion for her subject in her students at a large, inner-city school. But she just couldn't get them interested. She knew her subject inside out, she prepared her lessons thoroughly, she was keen and enthusiastic – but her classes just never took off. Henry VIII, the Armada, even Hitler and the Nazis – everything went down like a lead balloon. Two weeks into her teaching practice she was wondering if she should give up and do something else. In despair, she opened up one lunchtime to Matt, head of the English Department.

'Have you heard of Paddy Chayefsky?' he asked. Katie shook her head. 'Famous film writer,' said Matt. 'Won three Oscars. He once said, "First you have to make an audience care. Only then can you bother them with facts." It's the same with the kids. Why should they care about anything we're saying? Crack that and you'll be off and running.'

That night Katie thought hard about what he'd said and realised what she'd been doing wrong – she thought history was really interesting so she assumed her students would find it really interesting too. But now, looking through their eyes, she saw that what she was teaching was simply too remote from their everyday experience.

In her very next lesson she changed her approach. Henry VIII wasn't a Tudor monarch but the head of a nationwide criminal gang, ruling through fear and favours, and showing off his wealth and strength at every turn to remind everyone exactly who was boss. The kids loved it. And just as Matt had said, from that moment she was off and running.

Katie's teaching practice really took off when she switched her focus from transmission – what she was saying – to what her students could actually receive. She realised, in effect, that she'd been transmitting in FM to radios that were tuned to AM. And once she made 'being understood' her priority she started transmitting on the right wavelength. This didn't mean that the substance of what she was teaching changed, simply the manner of its delivery.

> **Don't appear so scholarly, pray. Humanise your talk and speak to be understood.**
> *Molière*[1]

Making 'being understood' our priority means taking responsibility for the listener's understanding, rather than taking it for granted – 'I've told them, so that's my job done.' It means being open, in that moment, to any possible questions and challenges that might arise; and it can demand, in that moment, the creativity of finding new, freshly-minted ways to describe things.

And regardless of the subject, the occasion or the relationships involved, being understood is fundamentally about serving basic human needs, on both sides of the process. For the 'transmitter' it could be the need for expression, to be understood, to be heard, to get a job done or simply to talk something through to get their own thoughts clear. For the 'receiver' it could be the need for sense, for clarity, for order, for respect or consideration. There are many possibilities. But whatever the subject and whatever the relationship, the way we express ourselves will succeed or fail depending on the extent to which we meet the human needs of those involved. Consider this fictional scenario.

Claire, 34, had recently started working in LCT, the family tool-making business founded years ago by her dad, Larry. Claire's role was to develop the website, marketing and distribution, with a long-term view to taking over the firm; but her greatest challenge was her relationship with her dad, an old-school engineer who 'led from the front' and 'didn't suffer fools gladly'.

One Friday afternoon Larry stormed into Claire's tiny office, a sheaf of papers in his oil-stained hand.

'These people drive me crazy,' he fumed. 'How am I supposed to run a business when they keep chopping and changing?'

Claire looked up from her computer, confused. But before she could say anything...

'Three months – that's how long that stupid woman's been umming and aahing. And now this!' Larry slammed the papers onto Claire's desk. 'She wants it all next week – the whole lot! God knows how many times I've explained things to her, but it's like talking to a brick wall.'

Claire started flicking through the now-grubby pages, trying to make sense of things. 'Well, maybe we can sort something out.'

'Yeah – I'll sort her out! I've had enough.'

Larry snatched the papers from under Claire's nose and stomped out.

'Whoa, Dad – hang on! Don't you think we should –'

But Larry was already halfway back to his office. Claire jumped up and dashed after him, anxious to stop him alienating yet another customer.

So – did Larry make himself understood? Well, up to a point, yes. Claire understood that he was angry and frustrated, and that he was about to give a customer a piece of his mind. And maybe she guessed that the problem was something to do with an order. But beyond that? What were his needs and what were hers? And how were they met – or not? Here are some possibilities.

Larry needs order, efficiency and consistency to run his business and, by failing to understand and observe LCT's ordering system, 'that stupid woman' (he doesn't even name her) is not meeting these needs. Larry can't understand why he's not connecting with her – 'it's like talking to a brick wall' – and needs to express his frustration by venting at someone, so he needs the attention and connection with Claire, who is both nearby and safe. But this doesn't meet his need for effectiveness and resolution – that is, it doesn't solve his problem – so he decides to sort things out by challenging 'that stupid woman' directly.

Claire needs order too, as well as peace and harmony, so that she can do her work. But these needs are blocked the moment Larry enters demanding her attention – which means her needs for respect and consideration are not met either. Like Larry, Claire also has a need for understanding – what exactly is the problem that's triggered him and what exactly does he want from her? She guesses that he wants help to find a solution – 'Well, maybe we can sort something out' – but at no point does Larry actually express a need for help or support. In essence, he wants an audience to help him gather his thoughts and feelings before confronting the 'enemy' – which will meet his need for resolution. But this will deny Claire's need for harmony and effectiveness – she wants to meet the needs of 'that stupid woman' too (though she almost certainly doesn't see her that way), and to nurture this customer-supplier relationship – so she rushes out after Larry to try to stop the imminent fireworks.

As this example shows, a lot of basic needs can be packed into even a brief exchange involving only two people, and a failure to be understood in that moment can mean most – if not all – of these needs will be unmet, with who knows what consequences.

HELPING OTHERS UNDERSTAND

Fortunately, there are some simple actions we can take to help others understand things in a way that meets the needs of everyone involved. While many of us do some or all of them as a matter of course, being understood in a creative conversation involves three basic elements.

- **Setting up** – preparing the listener to receive what's coming by stating what we want to talk about (the *Headline*) and why (our *Purpose*).
- **Painting a picture** – transferring what's in our mind into the mind of the listener as if we're painting a picture, giving a clear *frame* and enough *background* and *foreground* details for them to make sense of what they're hearing.
- **Checking** – ensuring that the listener has properly 'received' (i.e. understood) what we're trying to transmit

One way of looking at it is to think of the process as a sandwich – the first and last elements are the slices of bread, and 'painting the picture' is like creating the filling in the middle. As Figure 5.1 shows, the sandwich filling can be made up of all kinds of interesting ingredients, but it needs to be held in place by the more straightforward bits of bread above and below.

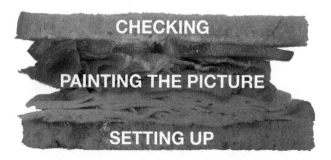

Figure 5.1 The 'Being Understood' sandwich

Likewise, setting up before we start to paint the picture, and checking afterwards, gives a structure to what we want to say that helps our listener take it in and understand it as whole. To put it another way, if the bread weren't there the filling would simply be a collection of ingredients that would be a lot messier to eat.

To see this in action, here's an alternative version of the conversation between Larry and Clare which leads to a different outcome. Larry is still brusque and annoyed but, using the three elements above, he helps Claire to understand – and so helps himself in the process.

Larry stormed into Claire's small office, a sheaf of papers in his oil-stained hand. 'These people drive me crazy,' he fumed. 'How am I supposed to run a business when they keep chopping and changing?' Claire looked up from her computer, confused. 'Ah, sorry, Claire,' said Larry, 'You in the middle of something?'

[Larry realises he's just barged in on Claire and demonstrates a bit of conversation management by apologising and checking that it's OK to talk.]

'It's fine' said Claire, saving her work and turning to face him. 'I'm all ears.'

'OK.' Larry took a deep breath. 'We've got a big challenge with an order from Meadvale and we've got to come up with some options, because I'm going to have to call them back before the end of play.'

[Larry then **sets up** what he wants Claire to understand by putting his main point up front and centre in a bold, clear statement – 'We've got a big challenge with an order from Meadvale' (*Headline*). And he also lets her know what he hopes to get from the conversation – 'We've got to come up with some options' (*Purpose*).]

'*OK...*'

[So far, so good. With her 'OK' Claire signals that she's paying attention and is ready to receive the main message. But Larry doesn't assume that she knows the history with this customer and the significance of this order, so he starts to **paint the picture** by first giving a clear *frame*.]

'*The thing is, they haven't used us for a while, for various reasons I won't bore you with, but this could be good news.*

[He thinks this could be a good opportunity and wants to focus on it. He then fills in some *background* information.]

'*The problem is Willie James, the owner, he's made a lot of changes there, like this new Head of Procurement – Brenda Cooper – and to be honest I'm not sure she's got a handle on how we work.*'

'*Why?*'

[With Claire now fully engaged and asking questions to help her understand, Larry sees she needs more *background*.]

'*Well, she made an enquiry about a big order – a range of cutters, bespoke, 200k – about six weeks ago and I told her we could do it by the end of this month if she confirmed within a week. Then zip – silence.*'

[And only then, having given her the background context, does he zoom into the key *foreground* detail.]

Till just now, an email pings up saying she wants to go ahead – but with the same delivery date, Friday week! You see the problem?'

[And note that he ends by asking Claire a question that prompts her to show she understands (**Checking**).]

'Absolutely,' said Claire. 'There's no way we can do it by then.'

[Bingo. Claire's concise summary means that Larry can continue, confident that they both have the same basic picture in their heads.]

'Exactly,' said Larry. 'So here's my thinking...'

In this short exchange Larry utters just a few sentences, which take only a minute or so, but Claire feels considered and respected, she's clear about the subject and what kind of contribution Larry is looking for from her. And with both of them now looking at the same picture, they can work together to solve the problem.

The three elements of being understood that Larry brought into play are effective precisely because they directly address the key needs of both parties – on his side, to be understood; and on Claire's, to understand. Let's look at them in more detail.

SETTING UP

The set-up helps our listener tune in to what we want to talk about and why.

Our **headline** states the main point we want to make in a short, unmistakable sentence that leaves no one in any doubt – just like the headline in a newspaper. And it's helpful to think in precisely these terms – 'What's my headline? 'What's my main point?' Without a headline, we can easily leave the other person (and indeed ourselves) stranded, with no idea of what this conversation's really about. Coming up with a headline and stating it clearly upfront addresses everyone's need for clarity and focus.

To be effective, a headline needs to be brief, clear and concise. 'I think I deserve a pay rise'; 'I'm worried about uni'; 'I want to go on holiday without your father.' None of these statements leave anyone in any doubt as to our view. There, we've said it – and the conversation can begin. And if we don't know what we think or are in a fog of confusion? Well, we just make *this* the headline. 'I really don't know what to think about...'; or simply 'I'm confused.'

Our **purpose** clarifies why the conversation is taking place and what we want to get out of it – 'I want to talk to *you* because...' – which helps the listener frame their response, since they now know where the conversation is going and what's expected of them. Without Larry stating his purpose, for example, Claire might have thought he wanted sympathy; or he might have been leading up to asking her to work all weekend; or...well, what? In the first version of their conversation, Claire has to guess what Larry wants – and guesses wrong. He abruptly rejects her offer of help because, in truth, he simply wants to vent his frustration before making a call. In the second version, though, Larry makes his purpose completely clear – and Claire responds by showing her understanding.

As with the headline, then, the purpose needs to be expressed clearly and concisely. 'I think I deserve a pay rise – and I want to explain why'; 'I'm worried about uni – and need some advice'; 'I want to go on holiday without your father – but want to know what you think.' And if we're looking for clarity, say so – 'I'm confused – and want to talk things through to get my thoughts straight.'

The key point is that by giving the headline and purpose (either of which can come first), the set-up helps the listener tune in to what this conversation is about and what we want from it. Which then gives them the freedom to choose whether or not to join in.

'I want to go on holiday without your father but want to know what you think.'

'I think... that's a conversation you need to have with Dad.'

PAINTING THE PICTURE

Next comes the core of what we want to say, the 'filling' in the sandwich. Painting the picture is a fluid process that involves transmitting to the listener anything that we think will help them understand what we're trying to convey. The story, facts, figures, reasons, examples, analogies, anecdotes, opinions, feelings and needs – anything can be included as long as it's relevant to the subject at hand and tailored to the needs of the listener. Quite how much information any individual listener might need is a matter of judgment – too little and they could be trying to make sense of a jigsaw that has more gaps than pieces; too much and they'll be overwhelmed, as if trying to put together a thousand-piece puzzle with no picture on the box lid to guide them.

To paint a picture that can be most easily understood by the listener, it's helpful to think of all these different types of information as serving three distinct functions – **framing**, **background** and **foreground**.

Framing is the process of setting the boundaries of what we want to say. Everything inside the frame is relevant; everything outside is not. Framing is a highly effective way of expressing what we think is important. To demonstrate, take a look at the following images.

Figure 5.2

Figure 5.2 hows some people looking out to sea on a bright, sunny day. In the middle distance is a sailing boat and beyond that the background of sea and sky, with a few more sails just visible on the horizon. This is what is known in film and

Figure 5.3

photography as a wide-shot, which typically shows the whole of its subject within a specific setting. Frame the scene differently, however, and the emphasis changes.

Figure 5.3 contains exactly the same basic elements as the previous image but by 'tightening the shot' – focusing more closely on some features and excluding others – a stronger relationship between the man and the closest sailing boat is implied. In Figure 5.2 it's just part of the scenery, while in Figure 5.3 the man seems to be focusing on it for some reason.

The framing of the image in Figure 5.4 tightens the shot even further. Again, a different understanding is formed in the mind of the viewer by what is included and excluded from each image. Without the context available in the previous two images, the sailing boat could be anywhere.

Figure 5.4

Framing functions in a similar way when we convey information through the spoken word. In essence, it sets the agenda by including what we think is important and excluding (if only by implication) what we don't. So the way in which we frame something has a major bearing on how a conversation develops. Look at these paired statements.

'I think I deserve a pay rise and I want to explain why. This isn't about the rights and wrongs of moving me to a new role. We've discussed that. It's about the fact that my workload's practically twice what it used to be.'

'I think I deserve a pay rise and I want to explain why. Travis gets way more than me and I don't think it's fair.'

* * *

'I'm worried about uni and need some advice. I'm not struggling with the work or anything – far from it. It's just that everything's getting messed up with politics.'

'I'm worried about uni and need some advice. 'Cos the debt's piling up and I know all that stuff about becoming a well-rounded person and everything, but right now I need to talk about where this is going – moneywise.'

* * *

'I want to go on holiday without your father but want to know what you think. I mean, I love him to bits but he never wants to go anywhere – and I do.'

'I want to go on holiday without your father but want to know what you think. I mean, it could be the last straw – which would obviously affect you...'

Each pair of examples above has the same headline and purpose, but the different framing indicates that a totally different conversation is on the cards. For example, *'I love him to bits but he never wants to go anywhere – and I do'* signals that the speaker doesn't want to focus on how she feels about her partner but on her unmet needs for variety and novelty. While *'it could be the last straw – which would obviously affect you'* signals that the focus will be a possible relationship breakdown and its fallout; the frame is being set wide enough to embrace both aspects.

Framing is a powerful technique to help others understand what we want to concentrate on (and what we don't), which can be very useful in preventing conversations shooting off in all directions or going over old ground yet again. But framing can also be a barrier to creative conversation if our frame is too rigid. Often, something of value is created in a conversation by *reframing*; that is, by allowing the frame to be adjusted to help one or both of the parties see something differently, or to accommodate what they both feel to be relevant and important. 'It might help to step back and look at the bigger picture' – so we pull out *together* to examine the wide-shot, the bird's-eye view. 'Yes, but what we mustn't overlook is…' – and we zoom in *together* to study a close-up on some detail, the frog's-eye view. In short, some degree of flexibility in framing is important.

The greatest difficulty arises when rigid frames clash; when the parties frame different aspects of the scene but refuse to accept that they're part of the same picture. 'Figure 5.2 shows some holidaymakers at the seaside' – full stop. 'No, it shows a boat on the ocean' – full stop. 'No, it shows a man wishing he could escape on a yacht – how could it be anything else?'

This is similar to the old story of the six blind men who encounter an elephant for the first time. One blind man grabs the trunk: 'An elephant is like a large snake,' he says. Another blind man feels its ear and says 'No. An elephant is like a kind of fan.' A third blind man touches its leg. 'Nonsense,' he says. 'An elephant is like a tree-trunk'; while a fourth blind man, feeling its side, announces that 'It's like a wall.' 'No, no, no,' says the fifth blind man. 'An elephant is hard and smooth, like a spear'; he was feeling its tusk. And the last blind man grabs hold of its tail and declares 'You're all wrong. An elephant is like a rope!' We can all see the absurdity of the blind men each insisting on the accuracy of his description of the elephant – until we ourselves insist on the truth of our particular frame.

Political, religious and cultural ideologies are often associated with inflexible, dogmatic frames, but our personal preferences can be just as powerful in consistently rejecting ways of framing that somehow don't chime with our basic values. For example, some people trust their intellect ahead of their emotions and tend to frame issues in terms of rationality, cost-benefit analysis and calculation. Others are the exact opposite – they believe that their emotions are the true and authentic guide to any issue, which 'cleverness' threatens to confuse or even bamboozle. Because didn't someone famous once say, 'I can prove anything by statistics – except the truth'?[2]

So in seeking to be understood, once again we can take full responsibility for *both* sides of the conversation by becoming aware of and challenging our own framing rigidities – as Angie did, for example, when she sat down to eat home-shot venison with her boyfriend's dad, Pete. Put simply, we're more likely to foster connection and the emergence of something of value in a creative conversation if we accept the need for flexibility in our own framing, regardless of the other person's frame.

* * *

The way we frame something also determines the nature of the information within the frame. **Background** detail describes or explains the circumstances (or terms) relevant to what we want to talk about, so that it can be fully understood by the listener as we see it; while **foreground** information is the main thing we want the listener to focus on. For example:

'I'm worried about uni and need some advice. (**Set up**)

'I'm not struggling with the work or anything – far from it. It's just that everything's getting messed up with politics. (**Frame**)

'For example, I'm doing this paper on the development of the novel and these activists have been physically disrupting the course because it focuses on "dead white guys", which they say is racist and sexist. And then you've got the alt-right protesting that Islam is getting special treatment on campus. And no one controversial is allowed to come and speak in case someone gets offended and kicks off. And the academics – they either support it or won't do anything, because anyone who opens their mouth gets trolled on social media in such a vicious… It's disgusting. (**Background**)

'So what do I do? You try to fight this stuff and woo – you're asking for trouble. But keep your head down and it just goes on and on. And I'm paying all this money – for what?' (**Foreground**)

If the difference between the frame, the background and the foreground is not clear, try reading the passage above with one of the elements missing. Without the frame, the full significance of the other information tends to be lost. Without the background, the other information feels 'unmoored'. And without the foreground, the background information feels incomplete – there's no 'hook' to get hold of. Leave out a couple of the elements and the meaning is almost wholly lost – to understand the listener will have to start asking questions to fill in the missing gaps. Only with all three elements does the full meaning of what the speaker is trying to convey become clear.

Of course, not everything we want others to understand has to follow this template. Generally speaking, the simpler the message, the less it's needed. For example, Figure 5.2 – the wide-shot – is quite a complex scene, so framing, background and foreground can help us in painting the picture. But the image of the sailing boat in Figure 5.4 is much simpler; in fact, the background seems barely relevant as the framing emphasises the foreground to the exclusion of everything else. So with relatively simple issues we can often get straight to the main point – 'Your father and I are going away for the first two weeks of August and we'd like you to feed the cats – OK?' Whereas a story like the one above about university politics needs more structure to help the listener understand.

In the end, exactly how we paint the picture is determined by how sensitive we are to the listener's response and can obviously be adjusted as the conversation demands. Framing, background and foreground can be useful tools; but the key is to continually bear in mind how we're being understood, so that the needs of the listener are never far from our thoughts.

> A genius knows how to make himself easily understood
> without being obvious about it.
>
> *Jean Anouilh*[3]

CHECKING

Keeping the listener's needs in mind means that it's useful to build **checking** prompts into the process of telling and being understood. 'Do you see?' 'Am I making myself clear?' 'Does that make sense?' – phrases like these offer the listener the opportunity to respond to what we're saying. And as they show how much (or how little) they understand, we can adjust the foreground or perhaps add more background until they do.

Simple 'yes' answers (or equivalents – nods or grunts) should be treated with caution, however, as for a whole variety of reasons people will often say they understand when they don't. So sometimes a direct request for feedback might be necessary, depending on the situation – 'This is really important, so can I just check what you've understood from what I've said?'

But checking isn't just a one-way process. It can also be incredibly useful in helping us to achieve clarity and understanding if we're confused or unsure about something ourselves. By prompting the other person to describe what they have or haven't understood, *we're* prompted to become more precise and clearer in our thinking and telling, especially if they're *not* grasping whatever it is we want to share. In effect, we can turn the other person into a 'sounding-board-plus' – an 'understanding-board'. In focusing on being understood by them, we can understand better ourselves, too.

Back at LCT, things have progressed. Larry has just outlined his plan for dealing with the problem order from Meadvale.

'So what do you think?' Claire looked thoughtful. Larry sensed she wasn't convinced. 'OK. Play it back to me.'

'Well, you're going to talk to the guys downstairs and see what they can do by next Friday. Then you're going to call your old mate Willie, blame his new Head of Procurement for not getting back to you in time, and see if you can negotiate a realistic delivery date with him.'

'Eh? I never said I was going to blame Brenda.'

'No, but by going over her head – or behind her back, she'd probably say – it has the same effect. It drops her right in it and next time – well, is she going to use us if she gets the choice?' It was Larry's turn to look thoughtful. 'Or – you could work it out with her directly, maybe. Diplomatically. Build a relationship.'

Larry looked hard at Claire, then smiled. 'I always said you had your mother's brains.'

He picked up his papers and headed back to his office.

Larry lays out his plan, prompts Claire to say what she's understood – and gets an unexpected bonus. Not only does she understand, she sees what he can't; namely that he's failed to take into account the wider effects of his actions – how Brenda will feel and how that might affect her attitude to doing business with LCT in the future. Claire is probably well aware of her father's blindspots (it might be one of the reasons why he's brought her into the firm); but the key point here is that Larry has the wit to *prompt* Claire to share her understanding of what he's said. She might have done so anyway, but when there's a power or status imbalance in a relationship it's far from guaranteed that anyone junior will speak up – witness Kara's story at the beginning of this chapter.

So try to build checking prompts into being understood – it's a very useful habit to develop.

BEING UNDERSTOOD WITHIN A CONVERSATION

There is a coherent order to the sequence explained here – Setting up, Painting a Picture, Checking – which, in reality, is often only possible if we're initiating the conversation. Assuming we've done our conversation management well and chosen the right time and place, we can exercise a certain degree of control over how to start things off. And generally speaking the sequence unfolds in this order because it helps the listener (and us) to focus on and understand what we want to say in a logical progression.

'I want to talk about [a] and I want your attention because of [b]. This [c] is the focus of what I want to say, this [d] is the background you need to know, this [e] is my main point – and now show me that you understand.

But what happens if we haven't initiated the conversation – what then? Maybe we're confronted with something totally unfamiliar, or have never even thought about – does this sequence still hold?

The short answer is that all the elements are still highly relevant – but not necessarily in the same order.

Over lunch, Rahit has poured his troubles out to his friend Ajay. They're not that close but Rahit values Ajay's calm and measured approach to life's challenges. Using his understanding skills, Ajay gets a clear picture of Rahit's situation and then sums up.

'So – you're being sued; you've found a good lawyer who's prepared to represent you at a fraction of her normal fee but it's still really pricey for you; she's urging you to settle because otherwise you might lose your house; but that means, in effect, admitting you're in the wrong –'

'Which I'm absolutely not.'

'Right. But you've got a wife and two young kids to think about, plus how all this is going to affect your career.'

'That's about it. Total mess. So what do I do? What would you do*?'*

Ajay thought for a moment, then sucked his teeth. 'Well, my honest response is – I don't know. I'm not a lawyer, I've never been in your situation, and from what I've seen of things like this... they can eat you up. Not just your finances, but your relationships, your health, your mental health.'

'I know.'

'My uncle went through something like this and the only people I saw who came out of it with anything positive were the lawyers. But maybe we can just talk through your options; get some clarity on what you care about and in what order. How does that sound?'

'Yeah. That would be helpful. Thanks.'

After confirming the accuracy of Ajay's summary, Rahit puts him on the spot – what would *he* do? And rather than blag an answer as a natural reflex to help his friend, Ajay gives an honest **headline** – 'I don't know.' He then gives some **background** that explains his basic attitude – he has no direct knowledge to draw on but has witnessed his uncle's experience. So he offers to continue the conversation by **framing** it with a different **purpose** – to help Rahit explore his options and clarify his priorities. And he then **checks** whether Rahit understands and accepts that new purpose. Rahit does – and the conversation could then continue by digging into the **background** and **foreground** of what he cares about and why. If Rahit had rejected that purpose, however, the conversation would have taken a different turn – or perhaps come to an end. The point, though, is that by stating a clear headline and offering some explanatory background, Ajay sets the conditions that allow the purpose of the conversation to be negotiated to his and Rahit's mutual satisfaction.

HITTING THE RESET BUTTON

These elements can also be useful to help reset a conversation if we start to lose our way.

'I'm sorry – I've lost my thread here. (**Headline**)

'*Why are we talking about this again? Wasn't it because...?*' (**Purpose**)

'*Sorry, I think we're going off-track a bit. What I want to focus on is....*' (**Framing/Reframing**)

'*Actually, there's a bit of context that would probably help here.*' (**Background**)

'*I suppose what I'm really trying to say is...*' (**Foreground**)

'*I'm not sure I'm really making myself clear. What are you hearing?*' (**Checking**)

In other words, even when we've not initiated the exchange, or when there's no initial clarity as to the *substance* of a conversation, or we start to lose the plot, by using these elements we can always have clarity about the *process* and get (back) on track to being understood.

So just to recap...

1. The key to being understood is 'empathic expression'; that is, to be aware that we're most effective as talkers when we can hear ourselves with the ears of those listening to us.
2. The 'Being Understood Sandwich' can help us give clarity and structure to what we're saying. After using a bit of conversation management to check that this is a good time and place to talk:
   - **Set up** with a clear, simple *headline* and *purpose* for the conversation
   - **Paint the picture** using *framing*, to clarify our basic approach and attitude, including what we think is relevant to this discussion; *background* to give context details; and *foreground* to highlight the main points

- **Check** that the listener has actually understood what we're trying to convey
3. The same basic elements can be used out of sequence even if we don't initiate the conversation and/or to get a conversation back on track.

* * *

The Three Practices of Understanding, Challenging and Being Understood deal with the practical, nitty-gritty of creative conversation. They focus on how, in our everyday exchanges with other people, we can put into action the spirit of the Three Principles – taking personal responsibility, staying open and being creative. And all Three Practices serve and support the relationship between those involved. Whether we're understanding, challenging or being understood, we're trying to stand alongside the other person and seeking to consider the same picture from the same point of view – not yelling across a canyon at each other while focusing on different aspects of the same scene.

But just as 'you cannot step twice into the same river',[4] so no two conversations are ever the same; each one requires a fresh, differently-blended approach to meet the needs of all the participants. So how do we go about making the decisions that will ensure that the right conversation is taking place in the right way with the right people, at the time and place most conducive to achieving a good outcome?

These questions are discussed in *Part Three – Application*, which starts by exploring that aspect of ourselves that's always running in the background, monitoring how our interactions with other people are going – our 'Conversation Manager'. Conversation Management plays a vital role in creative conversation, so let's look at what can happen when it's handled well – and what could go wrong when it's not.

Part Three

Application

Part Three discusses how to apply the Three Principles and Three Practices in various day-to-day situations, particularly where creative conversation might seem difficult or even impossible.

Chapter 6: Conversation Management looks at ways to develop an awareness, moment by moment, of how best to guide any conversation we have towards creating 'something of value'.

Chapter 7: Why don't we talk? takes six common obstacles to creative conversation and offers ways to overcome them.

Chapter 8: So what now? looks at what you can do to start your very own talking revolution the moment you finish reading this book.

Chapter 6

The Conversation Manager

Talking is a messy business. We blurt things out, change tack, go off on tangents, lose the thread, forget things, use the wrong words, leave important things out, interrupt each other, talk over each other, get the wrong end of the stick, don't say what we really mean, often don't even finish our sentences – there are so many imperfections in the way we communicate it's surprising we ever understand each other at all. But that's what comes with the spontaneity of conversation – which can also spring all sorts of positive surprises and lead us into unexpected, unexplored and enriching places. Every conversation is different, made in the moment by everyone taking part – no one 'owns' it – and then it's gone, to live only in the memory (perhaps).

> **Conversation is a game of circles.**
> *Ralph Waldo Emerson*[1]

In a sense, everything in this book is aimed at bringing some degree of order to this messy, ephemeral business – but without killing its spontaneous, organic quality. It's aimed at fostering a self-awareness in how we talk and listen that doesn't impose a rigid formula on natural, flowing communication, so that creative conversation has the maximum chance to spark and flourish.

Part of this self-awareness involves recognising that in

any human interchange there are always unspoken thoughts percolating away beneath the surface that can greatly affect the outcome. Things like…

'Here we go again…'

'Wow – she really knows her stuff.'

'He's not listening to a word I say.'

'Hmm – that's a good point.'

'We haven't got time for this.'

'Oops – that didn't come out right…'

Thoughts like these often have nothing to do with the explicit subject of the conversation. They're all about its process – how it's going and how we see our role in it. While talking about whatever it is, we're also monitoring the mood, taking the emotional temperature, possibly keeping an eye on the clock; or maybe feeling intimidated, invigorated, bored, surprised, offended or any one of a thousand emotions.

MEET THE MANAGER

All of these factors are being clocked, moment by moment in the background, by an unseen and trusted, but rarely acknowledged, servant – our Conversation Manager. This powerful little Mini-Me basically decides who we talk to, about what, and whether, when, where and how. Our Conversation Manager might be working well for us – which is great – or he/she might habitually be making not-so-bright decisions that stop conversations (and relationships) developing their full bandwidth. Either way, by bringing our Conversation Manager out of the shadows and into the light we can become more fully aware of the 'operating system' that governs how we approach conversation – and take greater charge of it.

But this can be challenging. When we talk we're not used to thinking consciously about the process of our conversations as well as their content. The process is usually just intuitive, unconscious. And hands up – we, the authors, don't always practise what we preach (as our friends and families will testify). The more we personally care about something, the more riled we're likely to feel if we think that it's under fire in some way, especially if we're off-guard at the moment of attack. When we're 'ambushed by anger' or some other powerful emotion, all the creative-this and empathic-that can so easily start to go out of the window, and our thinking and behaviour revert to fight-flight-attack-defend-counterattack mode. This is one reason why steadily training our Conversation Manager is so useful – he or she can step forward and take control in that moment of ambush.

Shona was starting to feel irritated. She was facilitating a meeting about a new sales strategy she'd been working on for weeks and Bob was in the process of systematically taking it apart. Shona was generally OK with criticism of her ideas – she knew from experience that it often contained useful pointers for development. But here, it was obvious from everything Bob was saying that he was shooting from the hip.

'He clearly hasn't read the proposal I sent everyone last week,' she thought crossly, 'because I've addressed and answered every point he's objecting to.'

But Bob was an experienced and persuasive character, much respected by his colleagues, and Shona could see that he was turning the meeting against her ideas. So perhaps no one else had bothered to read her proposal either. No one was speaking up for it – that was for sure.

'Typical,' she said to herself. 'Why put in all that effort if no one cares enough even to bloody read it?'

Bob stopped speaking. It was her turn. She felt the muscles in her face tighten, her lips start to purse – signs she knew meant her anger was rising. Anything she said now was likely to come out sounding decidedly hostile. But then a little voice in her head suddenly said 'Summarise.' And she listened to it.

'So what you're saying,' she said, 'is that instead of targeting different market sectors in turn, we should look at where we are currently in each sector and how we can build from there in each one. It's getting to the same end point but by moving in parallel, not one sector after another.'

'That's a good way of putting it,' said Bob.

Shona looked round the room. Several heads were nodding.

'Hmm,' she said. 'Which could also be a good way to get everyone involved in the strategy from the outset.' She thought for a moment – with a change of emphasis her hard-worked-out ideas could still be highly relevant.

'OK – how about this?' She briefly outlined how her proposal could be adapted to embrace Bob's concerns.

'Brilliant,' said Bob. 'Let's look at the details.'

The little voice that told Shona to summarise was her Conversation Manager – who wasn't concerned with the *content* of what was being discussed but had been monitoring the *process* of the meeting from the beginning, ever-alert to the nuances of what was being said – and not said – by everyone there. Who recognised the tell-tale signs of Shona's anger and knew that expressing it wouldn't be the most positive or constructive way forward. Who also knew that Shona didn't *have* to defend her proposal or point out that it already anticipated everything that Bob had said – because her Conversation Manager knew that there was another option: 'Seek first to understand.' And her Conversation Manager was proved right, because once Shona had understood – as confirmed by Bob's reaction – she was able to reframe the problem in her own mind and offer a new solution that turned out to satisfy the needs of all present. Bottom line – Shona's Conversation Manager kept asking 'What does success look like here?' and so intervened at the crucial moment to transform a potentially negative situation into a positive one.

Shona's Conversation Manager is, of course, simply an aspect of her own consciousness, the part that has learnt not simply to *react* but to *respond*. Reactions tend to be impulsive, instinctive and emotional, while responses tend to be the result of thought, experience, training and awareness. Police officers, firefighters and ambulance crew are called 'first responders', for example, because they're trained to head into difficult and dangerous situations at precisely the moment that the 'first reactors' – the general public – are running in the opposite direction.

On a less dramatic level, when we learn to drive a car we're initially dominated by our reactions. We're nervous at being out on the road in charge of a powerful machine, surrounded by other powerful machines, and as a result will often *react* inappropriately – braking too hard or suddenly swerving when a car appears at the junction of a side street, say. But as we grow in confidence behind the wheel, thanks to the training we're getting and the experience of driving in traffic, increasingly we learn to *respond* to what's going on around us. When a car appears at a side street junction we might gently brake or, seeing that it's given way, simply drive on. And increasingly, we develop 'road-sense'; an awareness that enables us to anticipate a potentially dangerous situation and, almost without thinking, take the right action before it becomes critical.

Our Conversation Manager is like our road-sense, only applied to how we talk to each other. From Shona's experience, we can see that the Conversation Manager combines four powerful and related types of awareness – of self, of others, of situation and of the principles and practices of creative conversation. Shona's Conversation Manager showed:

- an awareness of her changing mood and how it might affect things if not checked
- a sensitivity to her colleagues in the meeting, Bob in particular
- an awareness of how the meeting was developing and the avenues it might take; and
- an awareness of one of the Three Practices – 'Seek first to understand' – which she demonstrated by summarising Bob's criticisms (Shona has had some creative conversation training)

Her Conversation Manager also showed an awareness of all of the Three Principles; that is, Shona took *personal responsibility* for moving the conversation in a positive direction and forced herself to remain *open* when she felt herself closing down, both of which enabled her to *create* a suggestion for a new way forward.

SETTING THE RIGHT CONDITIONS

The Conversation Manager doesn't just oversee the ins and outs of a creative conversation when it's in progress; they also have a hand in setting the right conditions for it to start on the best possible foundation. For example, our Conversation Manager might suggest we do a little mental pre-planning.

Do I want primarily to understand something? Or be understood? Or maybe just open up a subject and examine it together? Is there something I particularly want to challenge? Or do I want to be challenged – and how will I respond if I am?

Simple preparation like this that enables us to clarify our basic purpose can really help a conversation get off on the right foot. So can consulting Kipling's Six Honest Serving Men, described earlier – plus the honorary Seventh, Whether. In Chapter 4 we looked at them in relation to Challenging but they're also highly relevant to how we approach creative conversation overall.

Now, much of what follows comes pretty automatically to any capable Conversation Manager – which is to say that we don't have to ask all of these questions all of the time. Even so, it's worth considering each Serving Man in turn, as each has a particular contribution to make in setting the right conditions.

Who are we talking to?

It's such an obvious question that we don't always ask it. Often we don't need to – we know the person well. But with people who are less familiar to us, asking this question can be extremely helpful. Some people make a virtue of treating everyone alike and up to a point that's fair enough – there's certainly no downside, for example, to showing everyone respect and consideration. But beyond a certain point it's definitely a case of 'different strokes for different folks'. If we want to connect with others we have to know to some extent who they are or be willing to find out. We have to acknowledge their individuality and attune to their wavelength, as trainee teacher Katie realised in trying to interest her school class in Tudor history.

It's the job of our Conversation Manager to do this tuning in, sometimes subtly (through visual and verbal clues, for instance) and sometimes by asking direct questions – 'Tell me a bit about yourself'; 'What sort of experience have you had?' and so on. It also works the other way, of course – 'Let me tell you a bit about me and my experience.' The challenge is to find a wavelength that suits both (or all) parties to the conversation, which means trying to understand who they are.

This includes being sensitive to the cultural differences that might exist between us. Which doesn't just mean of nationality or religion but of region, class, education, age, gender, sexuality – anything, in fact, that either of us might take for granted that is actually done differently as a matter of 'cultural' course by the other person. For example, Pete, the gun-owning Kentuckian and Angie, his son's British girlfriend, clearly live in different cultures, but so – by the sound of things – do Pete and his son Josh. Showing genuine and respectful curiosity about how our cultures differ can also be a powerful way to connect.

Why are we talking?

The purpose of any conversation is often understood intuitively between people who are close, but as the communication/relationship distance grows the scope for possible misunderstanding increases. What is meant as banter or affectionate teasing by one person could be misconstrued as a pointed dig, or even bullying, by the other if the speakers don't know each other that well. So our Conversation Manager also has to judge, on a case-by-case basis, how important it is to clearly signal the purpose of a conversation if we're initiating it (or clarifying it if we're not). This means that it helps to be clear about it ourselves *before* we start talking – as flying instructors often tell their students when teaching them how to send radio messages, 'Engage brain before mouth.'

Even if we just want to chat or think out loud, or share an anecdote or experience or observation, we have to give the other person a reason to listen to us – or it's likely that their attention will wander. And as we saw in the Understanding and Being Understood chapters, when things are more serious and we need more focus it's essential to clarify upfront why we want to have this conversation. Naturally, our Conversation Manager can also seek to clarify the purpose of a conversation if someone else is kicking it off but we're a bit foggy about precisely why.

What are we talking about?

Again, much that's been said in the Understanding and Being Understood chapters is relevant to this question but, as applied to setting the right conditions, the Conversation Manager's task is to try to establish as early as possible the headline and framing – what's the subject of the conversation and what's inside the frame? This then helps our Conversation Manager gently keep 'discipline' during the conversation – 'Sorry, but how is that relevant?'; 'Erm, aren't we going a bit off-piste here?'; 'OK – but I thought we agreed we weren't going to talk about that.'

When are we talking?

The 'when' of talking obviously relates to time but is also relevant to situation and sequence. Taking them in turn: to maximise the chance for mutual understanding, we need to choose the time to talk when we have the greatest chance of grabbing the other person's undivided attention and vice versa. So making it a habit to check if 'now' is a good time for them to talk – and if not, when? – doesn't just show consideration; it also helps set the optimum conditions for a creative conversation. Similarly, letting the other person know if 'now' is or isn't a good time to talk – and being firm about it if you must – is also doing you both a favour, as you'll be much more receptive to whatever it is they want to say if your mind isn't half on something else. As we saw in the alternative scenarios at the tool-makers LCT, Larry interrupts Clare both times but in the first version he blunders on regardless, oblivious to her confusion, while in the second he checks that it's OK to continue and so has her full attention – which leads to a much better outcome.

'When' in the sense of situation and sequence means judging more broadly the best time for a conversation – for example, when we're relaxed on holiday and away from the pressures of the working week, so the conversation can stop and start and develop over a longer period of time. Or perhaps the opposite is the case – we really can't put this conversation off any longer as things will only get worse if we do. Or again, thinking of sequence, perhaps we can only properly talk about something *after* various other things happen or become clear; until that point all we can do in reality is speculate or worry. Once again, the key factor guiding our Conversation Manager's judgment of 'when' is how to shape things so that the best possible connection can be made with the other person.

Where are we talking?

The physical context of a conversation can play a big part in how we talk and listen to each other, and so can affect the degree to which we can understand and be understood by each other. Is the setting comfortable and private, for example, or noisy and full of people? Are we talking on our ground or theirs? Is the location formal or informal? And will we – or they – feel relaxed or tense, or maybe a bit vulnerable, even intimidated? Where a conversation takes place is not always important or something we can have much control over. But it's something our Conversation Manager should think about because it definitely matters.

For example, if the aim is to achieve complete mutual understanding, it might be best to have the conversation in a neutral space where nobody has an advantage. Choosing to talk in a bar or over a cup of coffee is stating that the conversation is going to be informal and – hopefully – friendly and relaxed; while arranging an exchange sitting across from each other at a board table (maybe with someone taking minutes or even recording it) is at the other end of the spectrum.

And then there's the occasion when someone demands our attention just where and when we don't want to give it to them. At which point our Conversation Manager needs to scan the situation and make a swift calculation – not just about whether this is an appropriate time and place for this conversation, but whether we're *both* in the right frame of mind for it. We might feel seriously annoyed at being put on the spot, for example, or feel completely unprepared. So can it be rearranged or is it better to deal with it now, if only in part?

Here, too, a useful guide can be to ask what circumstance best serves this conversation and what best serves this relationship, this connection? There is no right or wrong answer, simply a judgment made in the moment that will often only show its value once it's been made.

How are we talking? (aka Channel Choice)

In this context, the 'how' of talking doesn't refer to managing the ins and outs of a creative conversation, which are covered by the Three Practices. Rather, it's about setting the right conditions through what might be called 'channel choice'; that is, selecting which of the many communications channels that exist today for any particular exchange. These fall into several broad categories:

- Face-to-face
- Audio + video (phone/computer)
- Audio (phone/computer)
- Written messages (Snail mail, Email, SMS/text, Instant Messaging, Forums, Chatrooms)
- Social media (Facebook, Twitter, Instagram)
- Talking with pictures/mixed media (e.g. SnapChat)

All of these channels can involve two or more people, can be more or less private or public, and offer various pros and cons. For example, in a face-to-face exchange both parties can see each other's facial expressions and body language, hear the nuances of each other's vocal tones and speech patterns, and react in the moment to what is being seen and heard. All of this – which is lost in text-based communication – might be thought of as wholly positive, the gold standard of personal interaction, until the potential drawbacks are factored in. One person might feel awkward in the physical presence of the other, for instance; or be verbally dominated by them; or be affected by what they look like; or not trust their ability to control their emotions in the encounter; and so on.

A popular way of talking about something in each other's physical presence while avoiding these potential drawbacks is to go for a walk – sharing the experience of being in the same place at the same time, while also feeling free to not talk for a while if you don't want to. There's an ease of conversation that's often produced in situations like this, and many different ways to achieve it – gardening, decorating, cooking together, driving, playing games with children (or grown-ups). Any shared activity that provides room to think and talk can help us open up in ways that bring the possibility of gold-standard, face-to-face conversation that bit closer.

At the other end of the spectrum, thanks to the Internet we now have multiple opportunities to connect in real time with strangers across the world. Many of them will be wholly anonymous, many will not be entirely honest about who they are – and some of them might not even be human...

The basic point is that the medium or channel through which we communicate has a significant effect on how the exchange is both shaped (its form and content) and coloured (its feel). And because increasingly we 'talk' through a variety of channels – we might even mix them during the same conversation, texting someone while we're speaking to them on the phone, say – our Conversation Manager has to judge which channel (mix) is best suited for each exchange. Here's a typical (fictitious) dilemma.

Hannah is at work one afternoon when she's invited to a movie that evening by a colleague she really likes. She says yes – then realises it's Tuesday, the night she regularly visits her mum, who lives alone.

Hannah doesn't want to cancel her movie date, so immediately reaches for her phone to send her mum a text. At which point her Conversation Manager steps forward – is that the right channel? What are the options? Hannah could...

- *Send the text – something like 'Soooo sorry mumma, can't make tnite. Call u tomoz xxx.'*
- *Phone her mum and explain.*
- *Call round and see her mum quickly on the way to the cinema.*

As always, the best thing to do depends on the context. Hannah's relationship with her mum might be solid enough for a text to be OK and not cause upset – she knows her mum wants her to get out more and won't mind at all. Alternatively, she might have let her mum down a few times recently, which would load the situation very differently. In either case, choosing to send a text means that Hannah can't know her mum's immediate reaction because she won't be present when her mum reads it.

And if her mum chooses to text her back, the reply might be carefully worded to conceal her true feelings.

A phone call, however, means that Hannah and her mum will, at least, communicate directly. They'll hear each other's voices, sense each other's feelings and be able to respond genuinely there and then. So the phone call, while maybe more time-consuming, has more elements to it that can help establish mutual understanding and maintain a healthy relationship.

But perhaps Hannah's workload won't allow the luxury of a call, or she suspects her mum will be wounded and she really doesn't want to have that conversation while she's at work. So maybe popping in on the way to the cinema for a quick face-to-face might be best after all. Of course, face-to-face conversation isn't always practical either, or indeed necessary – '*Running late, b there in 10*' is fine in a text. But it all depends – and checking through the pluses and minuses of each channel is, in effect, what Hannah does with her Conversation Manager before making her choice; that is, *responding*, not *reacting* automatically by sending a text, just because that's what she always does.

Ideally, face-to-face is best. It conveys consideration, commitment and respect to the other person, and sometimes our physical presence alone can say that we think our relationship matters. But what's ideal in theory doesn't necessarily create the most value in reality.

Jordan's relationship with his father had been getting steadily worse for years. It was as if they were magnetically drawn to upsetting each other every time they spoke.

'*It got to the point where we could barely be in the same room together,*' said Jordan. '*Each time he spoke to me it was to have a dig – or at least that's how it felt – and I hardly ever spoke to him at all. Things got easier when I moved out, but it was a real test every time I wanted to see my mum. I'd promise myself not to lose my temper but time and again he'd say something that got under my skin and – well, I'd snap or end up storming out.*

'But it wasn't a good situation and as I thought about it I realised we'd just got into this pattern, this habit with each other when we talked, and it could either continue or be broken. We needed a reset but I knew if I tried to do it verbally we'd probably just fall into the same old routine.

'So I wrote him a letter. It took a while because I had to sort out exactly what I felt and thought, and I wanted to put it in a way that was honest but didn't point the finger, that just showed I wanted things to be better. And after about ten days I got a letter back. It was quite short but it said he wanted to make things better too. And then we started to talk again. It wasn't easy, but bit by bit we rebuilt things. Which made my mum happy. Well, all of us, really.'

When Jordan's intention changed and he started to reflect on his relationship with his dad, he realised that if they were going to reconnect he'd have to change channels. Talking face-to-face was just too emotional, too high risk, whereas writing a letter gave him the chance to be in full control of saying what he felt without being interrupted. And without knowing it, he naturally followed the Three Principles. He took *personal responsibility* for improving communication with his father; he *opened* up a new channel and was thus also able to *open* up himself in a new way; and through these actions he *created* the conditions for a better relationship, which benefited not just him and his dad but his mum as well.

Even so, changing channels was for Jordan ultimately a way to re-establish *face-to-face* communication with his father. That still mattered to them both because, when it works, talking and listening face-to-face offers the maximum possible bandwidth between people, the maximum possible understanding and the maximum possible connection.

> **That is the happiest conversation where there is no competition, no vanity, but a calm quiet interchange of sentiments.**
> *Samuel Johnson*[2]

THE COMMUNICATION LADDER

From this viewpoint, with every step down the communication ladder the bandwidth narrows. As we become increasingly disembodied – literally – one or more of the rich, relationship-enhancing benefits of face-to-face contact falls away.

Live video chats are arguably the next best thing to a face-to-face conversation. They have the advantage of visual and audio contact in real time but lack important aspects of physical interaction. We can't shake hands, for example, or give a comforting touch, offer a cup of tea, exchange objects or even see clearly what's going on around each other – our frame of vision is limited by the screen. So physical presence can offer a range of sensory advantages.

Next step down the ladder is the simple phone/audio call. This can offer a strong degree of connection because we're concentrated on the most agile and nuanced communication tool we have – our voices. And sometimes the lack of visuals can be a positive – in some therapeutic practices, for example, it's recognised that the less physical nature of a phone call can help people speak more freely and honestly. Ironically, though, in those therapeutic situations, the lack of meaningful human interaction can be a major part of the problem and getting back into engaging with other people face-to-face is part of the solution.

The communication bandwidth shrinks still further as

we descend the ladder to written messages. A simple rule of thumb is that the less physically present the participants are, and the less well they know each other, the harder the text has to work to ensure mutual understanding. This is because all the physical clues to meaning are absent and what's written becomes more open to misinterpretation (hence the increasing use of emojis to suggest tone and intention). Classically, for example, punctuation and layout can completely alter the sense of the text.

What's this thing called 'love'?

What's this thing called, love?

A woman, without her man, is nothing.

A woman – without her, man is nothing

What's that in the road ahead?

What's that in the road – a head?

Humour, too, is something that's often difficult to convey in written form, especially online, even at times with people we know well. Tone of voice, delivery, context, the knowing wink – all the hints are missing that 'this statement is not meant to be taken seriously'.

The difficulty of conveying intention is also one reason why meaningful and satisfying conversation is so challenging online. Another is that, as the participants often don't know each other, the standard considerations that we observe to protect our 'real' relationships – courtesy, politeness, respect – can be totally absent, often spectacularly so. From bluntness and rudeness through to outright hate-speech and even death threats – anything goes when the perpetrator can hide behind the anonymity of online connection. This is the basis of Godwin's Law,[3] first declared when the Internet was still in its infancy: 'As an online discussion grows longer, the probability of a comparison involving Hitler approaches 1 [i.e. certainty].'

On the plus side, written text offers a number of advantages, such as more control over when or whether to respond, and the ability to compose and recompose a message until its content and tone feel right (as Jordan discovered). Emails also give us a permanently stored and searchable record of what's passed between us, which can be invaluable (but not only to us if they're not encrypted). SMS/texting and instant messaging add the advantage of more immediate connection, although generally these channels are best reserved for those who know each other well enough to speak in a common shorthand.

Things are more complicated when it comes to social media platforms such as Facebook, Twitter and Instagram, as these online channels tend to blur the distinction between private and public space; at least, it seems, in the minds of many users. Content that's posted privately or to a restricted group might easily become public, for example, unless our privacy settings are correctly adjusted; if we're not careful a personal exchange with a friend might be seen by anyone who views our page or timeline. Writing text, posting images and sharing the content of others – many of whom we might not know personally – can become a minefield if we're not sure (or forget) for whom exactly we're doing this. Something that we share casually, without really thinking, or that's posted in the expectation that our friends will understand the intention behind it or recognise our tone of voice, can be seen by a stranger and interpreted in a completely different – and often hostile – way.

So, common to all communication channels that rely on written text (if only in part) is the point that we need to compose messages carefully, which means ensuring that what we're sending or posting is what we actually want the other person (or people) to receive and understand. If we don't, all kinds of costly misunderstandings could arise, which a phone call (if possible) – or even better, a face-to-face conversation – might have avoided.

In summary, then, when it comes to setting the best conditions for 'how to talk' our Conversation Manager needs a moment of orientation before we start. Are we in Understand, Challenge or Being Understood mode? And then, recognising the potential and limitations of each communication channel, which is the one that best suits the message *and* meets the needs of the people sending and receiving it? Ultimately, again, it all comes down to 'different strokes for different folks'.

✶   ✶   ✶

In time, with practice, our Conversation Manager will become as much part of us as road-sense becomes a part of a driver's consciousness. But, as with learning to drive, *intentionally* managing a conversation can feel clumsy and awkward at first.

As Figure 6.1 shows, we start at a point of *unconscious incompetence* – we don't know that we're lacking this particular ability. Then we move into *conscious incompetence* – we become aware of what we can't do. From there we progress to *conscious competence* – we start to develop this new ability

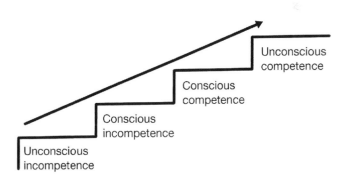

Figure 6.1 How to become unconsciously competent

but have to think deliberately about what we're doing as we've not yet mastered it. And then, in time, we reach a point of *unconscious competence* – we perform the skill smoothly, without thinking, and continually practise and refine it. Our Conversation Manager is fully integrated into how we think and act, always watchful but discreetly, in the background, like an attentive instructor. Even so, at crucial moments, they will spring forward to remind us of the Three Principles or the Three Practices, so that our conversation can be steered (back) in a positive, creative direction – as Shona experienced during her difficult sales meeting.

Whether to talk

Finally, we come to Kipling's honorary Seventh Serving Man – Whether. As with whether to challenge, whether to talk can be the hardest question to answer of all. One question to ask is 'How might my input help? What value will be created? Could it benefit the other person – or am I doing it just for my own sake?' Even then, so much depends on context. Not just of the moment, the present situation, but of the past and future too. Where does this exchange fit in relation to what's happened before? How will it affect what's to come? What could be not just the immediate impact, but the second-order, third-order and possibly further effects on this situation and this relationship – and maybe others?

That said, there are some generic situations where the problem of whether to talk or challenge typically arises. These are explored in the following chapter.

So just to recap…

1. The Conversation Manager is that part of our consciousness that both sets the right conditions for a creative conversation and monitors *process* – how the conversation is developing – so that we can maximise the chances that it will create 'something of value' for all involved.

2. A helpful way to do this is to use Kipling's Six Serving-Men:
   - *Who* are we talking to?
   - *Why* are we talking?
   - *What* are we talking about?
   - *When* are we talking?
   - *Where* are we talking
   - *How* are we talking i.e. which 'channel' is best for this conversation?
   - And also to consider the 'honorary' Seventh Serving-Man – *Whether* to have this conversation at all

3. The 'channel' through which we communicate has a significant effect on the form, content and feel of that exchange – communication bandwidth tends to narrow as we descend the 'communication ladder' from face-to-face conversation in the same physical space to reliance on text alone.

4. Increasingly, our conversations use both spoken words and written text and our Conversation Manager has to judge which channel mix is best suited for each exchange.

Chapter 7

Why Don't We Talk?

'To jaw-jaw is better than to war-war,' as Winston Churchill famously observed. It's a sentiment that most of us would heartily endorse – but in many situations we don't 'jaw-jaw'. Why not? Why don't we talk? What's stopping us?

One powerful reason is that we know from personal experience that talking alone doesn't automatically guarantee that things will get better; in fact, it might actually make things worse. So while the idea of creative conversation might sound lovely, what if…

… you just don't handle certain types of situations or people that well?

… you're stuck with someone who doesn't communicate brilliantly – or even at all?

… the culture of the organisation you're in means it's better just to keep your head down and get on with things, rather than voice your concerns?

Many of us have to challenge situations like these every day. Often, they can seem insoluble, especially if they've persisted for a while, and some communication problems do indeed last for decades – lifetimes even. But they don't have to.

This chapter looks at how creative conversation can help to

free up some of the typical situations that block so many people, families and organisations. At the heart of these obstacles is often the question that's been deferred till now – *whether* to talk or challenge; and if so, *how* in this specific situation.

The range of possible scenarios, though broad, can be grouped into three categories – '*the problem is me*', often centred on a lack of confidence; '*the problem is them*', where the obstacle is not our desire to engage but the negative reaction we get from others; and '*the problem is the situation*', which somehow seems to dictate how everyone behaves, even if everyone can see that it's far from ideal.

The categories aren't exclusive but overlap and influence each other; for example, someone lacking in confidence might be easily put off by another person's negative reaction or a situation that doesn't encourage communication. But whatever the mix, the principles and practices of creative conversation can help increase the bandwidth and resilience of personal, professional and societal relationships, no matter how deeply entrenched the problems within them may seem.

> **Mankind's greatest achievements have come about by talking, and its greatest failures by not talking.**
> *Stephen Hawking*[1]

It isn't a magic bullet, though. Just as medicine can't cure every ill, so creative conversation has its limits in repairing and improving communication and relationships – if only because sometimes 'the other side' will simply refuse to engage. So rather than being a cure-all, learning to use creative conversation is more like adopting a healthier lifestyle of diet and exercise that can benefit all areas of our lives. And looked at in this way, every one of the conversational issues discussed below can become the cause for healthier, more resilient relationships, now and into the future. Every positive effort we make to create 'something of value' in our interaction with another person will definitely make *us* stronger and more capable – whether we agree with them or not and however they choose to behave. This is cause and effect in action. There will always eventually be a positive effect on our lives if we make a positive cause. And sooner or later, it will bring clear, tangible benefit as well.

Bearing that in mind, let's consider a couple of common scenarios in each of the three problem categories.

THE PROBLEM IS ME

I don't want to look stupid… I'm scared about where talking might lead…

Lack of confidence in one form or another is a difficulty many of us share, however much we may like to pretend otherwise, and conversations often provide fertile ground for those anxieties of self-doubt to emerge, particularly with people we don't know well. But acknowledging that some of our problems with talking to other people are down to us is not a stick with which to beat ourselves – it is, in fact, the key to overcoming them. That's because the way we communicate is just a set of habits we've established over time, for one reason or another, and which we can therefore change. As with learning a musical instrument or any other skill, it's extraordinary how much more confident we can become after a bit of practice, and developing the skills of creative conversation is no different.

I don't want to look stupid

Let's say you're in a situation where someone says something you don't understand. If it's something you couldn't possibly be familiar with you'll probably feel OK about asking for some clarification. But if it's something you really should understand, what do you do – apart from silently panic? Bluff it out and hope the moment passes so your ignorance isn't revealed – or confess your confusion or ignorance in a responsible, open effort to stay on track, but risk as being seen as (maybe professionally) inept? This is a classic 'whether' to speak moment...

George was running a seminar for two hundred managers in education.

'Have any of you ever heard something in a professional setting you didn't understand and not *owned up to it?' he asked. 'Please put your hand up if you've* ever *done that.'*

Slowly, a sea of hands was raised.

'Well, I'm not surprised,' George continued. 'Keeping our confusion to ourselves is endemic. It's everywhere. You all work in education. You're meant to be inquisitive [the audience laughed] *but organisations of all kinds all over the country float on a sea of confusion because people don't want to look stupid. How stupid is that?'*

George went on to explain that he had for some years tried to operate a policy of zero-tolerance for confusion. It was hard for him, too, but it was paying great dividends.

'It can be embarrassing when you're meant to know something, or understand what's just been said, and you don't. I know that. But every time I raise my hand and confess my confusion – my stupidity, you might call it – I guarantee someone comes up to me afterwards and says thank you. Because they hadn't understood it either but didn't have the balls to say so. And all I did was say something like, "I know we've discussed this many times... but I'm still not 100% clear on what it actually

means." You can almost hear the silent sighs of relief round the table.'

'So what's more important?' he asked. 'Keeping everyone moving forward together and ensuring everyone's clear – or keeping up appearances? Which of those seems stupid to you?'

In other words, your uncertainty or ignorance can itself become the starting-point of a creative conversation, which you can frame in a way that states your needs and helps the other person meet them – 'I'm not sure of my ground here [*headline*] but I want to understand more about X [*purpose*].' Ironically, the moment you admit to uncertainty or ignorance is the very moment you open yourself up to all kinds of learning and insights that can lead to greater understanding – for yourself and others.

Of course, ideally you would then also address exactly *why* there was this gap in your understanding or knowledge in the first place...

I'm scared about where talking might lead

Creative conversation has the power to lead to greater mutual understanding – but there's no guarantee that this new understanding will be what you anticipated. A creative conversation with your spouse, for example, could lead to a deeper relationship – or to you both recognising that the marriage is over. A creative conversation with your boss could end with a better job – or maybe no job. A serious challenge to a dysfunctional organisation (aka 'rocking the boat') could lead to systemic change – or your ejection from the system.

So before deciding *whether* to begin any significant conversation it's worth contemplating a range of possible outcomes – best, worst and most likely, perhaps – and how you might deal with them. At the same time, it's also worth considering the consequences of *not* having that potentially scary conversation. Many relationships – personal, professional and societal – founder not because a problem is present but because communication is absent. This latter aspect can easily become the more corrosive, as illustrated in the tale of Stella and Mike, whose marriage broke up over his refusal to talk about her desire to take a degree course. No communication, no relationship.

In sensitive personal situations like this, there's great value in taking things one step at a time – using your Conversation Manager to set the best conditions for the exchange, then seeking to understand before seeking to be understood, striving to see the world through the other person's eyes, and articulating without judgment your understanding of what you've heard. Doing that, in and of itself, will reinforce the quality of any personal relationship and provide a more secure platform from which to take the next step.

This considered, step-by-step approach will also help you approach creative conversations that address thorny aspects of group and societal pain. Here, though, the situation can be complicated by the challenges of scale and power imbalances. How long might it take to bring about the change you want to see, for example? Are you prepared for the long haul, if necessary – and at what potential cost? We return to this issue towards the end of the chapter.

But whether your challenge is personal, group or societal, creative conversation can definitely help you move forwards. And if you're hesitant about the initial step, why not first have a creative conversation with a trusted friend or advisor, if you can? That way, you can get your thoughts into shape and some clarity about your options before broaching the subject with whoever, for you, is key.

THE PROBLEM IS THEM

The other person won't play... They never listen...

If lack of confidence is often at the heart of 'the problem is me', a sense of powerlessness is often at the heart of 'the problem is them'. And with this feeling of being unable to make things happen usually comes a combination of frustration, resentment, hopelessness and resignation.

'Why can't they see that...?'

'Why are they stopping me from...?'

'I'm going to be stuck with this forever.'

'Best just grit my teeth and get on with it.'

The bottom line to this reasoning is that 'they' have to change in some way for the situation to get better, or even for us to talk about it – a way of thinking that creative conversation fundamentally challenges.

The other person won't play

You want to talk about something that's important to you but the other person stubbornly, determinedly, refuses to engage – it's like getting blood from a stone. Or every time you raise the issue they get angry or take offence, thinking they're being criticised. Or they change the subject, or promise to talk about it another time (which never comes), or they find some other tactic not to talk. Whether they're doing it consciously or unconsciously, the end result is the same – you feel stuck. The important issue remains unexamined and unresolved, and at the same time your relationship is suffering, its communication bandwidth shrinking, almost as if it's being strangled. But no one is *obliged* to engage with you (unless there's some sort of legal requirement), so what to do? A good place to start could be to consider Aesop's fable of the Sun and the North Wind.

The Sun and the North Wind were fierce rivals, constantly vying to outdo each other. One day, they saw a traveller walking along the road and made a bet over who could remove his coat from him.

'Watch this,' said the North Wind, whipping up a fierce gale. But the harder it blew, the more tightly the traveller wrapped his coat around himself. Eventually, exhausted, the North Wind stopped blowing.

'My turn,' said the Sun, coming out from behind a dark cloud. It grew warmer and warmer, till the traveller started to perspire – and took off his coat...

Trying to force someone to change often has the opposite effect, whereas by changing the way *you* yourself think and act – by becoming more understanding, say, or more considerate – you change the dynamics of the relationship, to which the other person must then adapt, like the traveller voluntarily taking off his coat.

Joel was a successful entrepreneur who'd just sold the business he'd founded from scratch twenty years earlier. With plenty of free time to enjoy his new-found wealth at home with his wife and two teenage children, he knew he should be happy. But he wasn't.

'The big problem was me and my wife,' he said. 'Bit by bit our relationship had gone bad, to the point where the only stuff we ever talked about was who was going to put the bins out or do the school run, stuff like that. And me being at home more of the time had actually made things more difficult for us both.

'One time I tried to talk about our relationship but she didn't want to know, so I was forced to think about what to do. And as I reflected I started to notice things about myself, like how often I criticised people, either inwardly or to their face, especially my wife and kids. But I achieved very little by it other than to create a bad atmosphere no one liked – least of all me. Crazy, isn't it?

'So I decided to try an experiment. Without telling anyone, I decided to make a conscious effort for at least one week to curb the criticism. Just stop it – dead.

'At first it felt like a funny little game I was playing with myself, and so hard to do because I'm so critical. Swallowing my words and thoughts was really challenging. But as the days passed it got easier, so I just kept going.

'After about ten days, I was cooking in the kitchen with my youngest daughter and right out of the blue she said, "Daddy – you and mummy are getting on really well, aren't you?"

'I was so surprised I nearly laughed. But I didn't want to make too much of it, so I just kept chopping and said; "Are we? Yes, I suppose we are." I couldn't stop smiling, though, because she was right – my wife and I were getting on better. But I didn't own up to my little experiment.

'A couple of mornings later I was taking the kids to school, and as we walked out of the house I steeled myself for the inevitable squabble about which of them was going to sit in the front seat. But my older daughter simply said, "It's OK. I'll sit in the back today."

'I was amazed – she could normally conjure a row up out of nothing. Even more amazing was that the simple act of not criticising, and the unfamiliar appearance of a smile on my face, seemed to be having a positive effect on everyone.'

The key point about Joel's experience is that because *he* changed, not only did his relationship with his wife change but the dynamics of the whole family. And he made no announcement about what he was going to do – he just did it. Similarly, by applying the principles and practices of creative conversation, even unannounced, you can definitely change things for the better if the other person 'won't play'.

For example, if they refuse to engage it might be because they don't find it easy to express themselves, particularly when it comes to discussing anything emotional or contentious; in which case trying to make talking less daunting for them could be helpful. In fact, the practices of understanding outlined in this book were originally developed in the field of counselling psychology precisely to help people talk about things they found difficult to address. So paying attention, listening with an open mind, clarifying and summarising, and using TIPS when challenging, will all help the other person speak. You never know – it might be the first time they've ever been listened to in this way. And there's another bonus for you in situations where the other person is reluctant to play – they can stretch your ability to be responsible, open and creative to the limit, which is no bad thing.

It's also OK to be direct sometimes – to say that you can see it's difficult for them to speak about this issue and to be explicit about your reasons for wanting to bring it up. Using your Conversation Manager to choose the right time and place can make a big difference, too, as can talking while sharing an activity that brings you together in a non-confrontational way, such as walking or driving; something that minimises the tension and allows conversation to flow. This can also be especially effective with those who tend to get angry or irritated when you bring up a sensitive subject.

Speaking of anger, it's helpful to remember that the thing most likely to trigger it is if someone feels, rightly or wrongly, that something they care about, that they value, is being threatened or denied. So the key here is to stress to the other person that you value your relationship with them and want to maintain it; and that you want to address the issue at hand by first understanding them and what they care about, without threatening or denying anything. But if the anger or irritation still erupts, *that* is the issue that has to be addressed, as it will continue to block progress in this area – and probably in others, too.

The reality is that if your relationship is strong enough, if it has enough communication bandwidth, either party can say pretty much anything and be heard. But if your relationship is fragile, the smallest comment can potentially cause offence.

So practise on the small stuff, too. Use every conversation, however trivial, to build the communication bandwidth of all your relationships, so that when something is tough to say and, you think, could be tough to hear, the conditions are right for it to be understood in the spirit in which it was offered. In many ways it's your overall approach to the conversation, rather than any specific point you make, which speaks loudest – because your approach, your attitude, has nothing to do with the content but everything to do with the way you value the person in front of you.

184

They never listen

Not being heard can be very painful. Our fundamental human needs for acknowledgement, attention, consideration, recognition – all are being denied, so we can feel frustration, exasperation, hopelessness, even despair. And, very often, anger. Many conflicts, from the personal to the societal, can deepen and intensify if one or more of the parties judge that 'the other side' are deliberately not listening. It's clearly a vitally important topic – but what does the phrase 'they never listen' really mean?

For example, it could refer to someone who basically delivers a monologue every time they open their mouth. They seem to speak without drawing breath and our every attempt to interject just sets them off on a new, long-winded stream of consciousness. It's a case of 'transmitter up, receiver down' – a one-way, overwhelming flow of their thoughts, their opinions, their observations, their feelings and their judgments.

Paula, a highly experienced consultant in dialogue skills, was once invited to coach a senior executive of a large multinational corporation. On the appointed day she was ushered into the executive's spacious office, they shook hands, sat down – and the executive started to tell her what he thought about personal communication. At length. A couple of times Paula tried to say something but the executive just ploughed on. After a few minutes she decided she'd had enough.

'You have to stop now,' she said. He didn't. 'Please STOP!'

Startled, the executive stopped in mid-flow.

'Let me explain how this works,' said Paula. 'You say something, and then I say something, then you say something, and then it's my turn again, and so on. That's dialogue, OK?'

'Uh, yeah, sure,' said the executive. And then he carried on as if she hadn't spoken.

'No, no – stop again,' Paula said. And once again, the executive stopped in mid-flow.

'And when we take it in turns,' said Paula, 'what you say has to have something to do with what I just said, and then when I speak, what I say has to relate in some way to what you've just said. That's also key to dialogue.'

The executive thought for a moment, nodded, and the exchange resumed.

As this story demonstrates, sometimes the only way to counter verbal one-way traffic is to confront it head-on and politely demand that the rules of conversation be respected. "Enforcing dialogue' like this can be tricky, though,[2] especially when the culprit has a higher status than you or a direct challenge might only come at some cost.

'I' statements, one of Marshall Rosenberg's methods of nonviolent communication, can be effective here. The basic formula is 'When *A* happens, I feel *B* because I need *C*, so please could you *D*?' which in this case might translate into something like:

'When you're talking I honestly feel a bit overwhelmed because I need some space to properly engage with what you're saying. So maybe we could chunk these points up a bit and give ourselves a chance to discuss them together. How does that sound?"

Alternatively, you could double down on your Understanding skills and by trying that much harder – to pay attention, stay open, clarify and summarise – you could seek to make a real connection with the other person by breaking through their self-absorption. As well as helping you become a better Understander, these habits might also rub off on them. Many people have never been listened to in a respectful, non-judgmental way and might, therefore, simply not know how to do it.

However, 'they never listen' could mean something quite different – that for all the apparent listening being done by 'them' (partner, relative, employer, authority figure), you feel that your concerns haven't been properly recognised, let alone actually addressed. Here again, 'I' statements can help.

> *'When we talk and you say things like "What's the big deal?" or "You shouldn't worry so much", I feel frustrated and our relationship suffers. So when we speak, please could you acknowledge that what I'm saying is important to me, and respond by talking about it – even if you don't agree?'*

Two more points can also help greatly in these kinds of situations. The first is to be clear about what it is you want the other person to hear. 'You're not listening to me!' can be a cry of frustration when, for all our efforts, we sense that the real problem is actually that we're not being *understood*.

Could the PIN model help here? That is, are you clear about your Position – the facts of the matter, what you want to see happen or change? And/or do you want your Interests acknowledged – your feelings and what you care about – perhaps before any other details are discussed? And what about your underlying Needs – if you can identify and clearly express these, might you be heard at a different and potentially more creative level? Allying this model to the elements of Being Understood can be a powerful way of helping others to 'listen'; that is, understand.

The second point also relates to clarity – namely, to be as specific as possible when trying to get through those who 'never listen'. 'Never' and 'always' are words we often use in criticising other people – 'You never do this', 'You always do that' – but it's much more effective to give specific examples of what you're challenging.

> *'I've tried to talk to you about this three times in the past month. The first time you said you'd get back to me in a few days – but you didn't. The second time you said you were still thinking about it and the third time you just got angry. It's important to me, it's important to the group and I want to understand why you seem so reluctant to talk about it.'*

This example is quite confrontational – you can hear the frustration in the speaker's voice. But it is nevertheless specific and clear about what has happened and what the speaker wants – and note, again, the aspect of 'first understand': *I want to understand why you seem so reluctant to talk about it.*

The example also hints at a third possible meaning of 'they never listen' – the behaviour of those in positions of power and authority, often within a hierarchy, who are making (or just carrying out) decisions, policy or doctrine and are not accountable to anyone junior to them. They don't listen because they don't have to; or to put it another way, they listen only when they want or need to.

This can be infuriating, but for many people it's a reality of their everyday lives – at work, in their dealings with public bodies and other large organisations, and sometimes even in their families.

There is no straightforward remedy in these situations because the issue here is less about communication and more about power. How far are you willing to go to challenge it? Which of your needs are met by staying put and making the best of things, and which by trying to bring about change – or simply walking away? Only you can make that decision

– though even here, creative conversations with others can help you clarify your thoughts, feelings and options.

THE PROBLEM IS THE SITUATION ITSELF

It's gone too far... There's a power imbalance...

What do you do when the obstacles to communication seem to be beyond your control, the result of culture or history or structures for which no one feels directly responsible, but which still have a direct – and often negative – bearing on how people relate to one another?

Well, here too creative conversation can have a positive effect, not least because the first of the Three Principles – personal responsibility – means that you take it on yourself to create 'something of value' in each encounter you have with another person, in any situation. The key question then becomes what that 'something of value' is, and how much of it you can realistically create in different circumstances.

It's gone too far

For example, the phrase 'It's gone too far' or 'It's gone on for too long' often really means 'I've given up hope that this situation can ever be turned around.' And, often, that judgment is based on the fact that past sincere attempts to make things better – yours and/or theirs – have been rebuffed or unintentionally made things worse. You've tried your best and come to the conclusion that the current, adverse state of play is effectively set in stone.

Now, it's entirely possible that you and the other person (or group) are, in fact, irreconcilable. Your values and interests

– what you each care about – are so incompatible, or so much hurt has been experienced, that you'll both save everyone a lot of time and heartache by continuing to have as little to do with each other as you can.

But it's also possible that your judgment that 'it's gone too far' is simply wrong. With a new approach some kind of understanding might be reached, especially if underneath the hostility or coolness is a yearning on one side (or both) for things to be better – as Jordan discovered when he wrote his father a letter. In this case, the real questions are 'Do I acknowledge that yearning, that need for connection? And if I do, what am I going to do *differently* this time to bring it about?' In Jordan's case, he realised that he had to choose a different communication channel, so that he could express his sincere desire for a better relationship with his dad without the risk of being derailed by their mutual anger.

Once again, this is where your Conversation Manager can step forward. There's an old saying that 'A cave that's been dark for a thousand years can be lit with a single torch', and it's your Conversation Manager's task to decide exactly how the torch of creative conversation can light up this particular darkness.

The Three Principles, for example, mean that by deciding to take personal responsibility for the task you're also going to be open to what it demands, like not focusing upfront on issues of blame and right and wrong; and you're determined to try to re-establish, even if only in part, this broken connection.

Crucially, the most basic 'something of value' that needs to be (re)created in mending broken or unsatisfactory relationships is trust. And here it's important to recognise that trust is usually built step-by-step, over time. Quite how fast you'll be able to take those steps depends on several factors, not least how bad things truly are at the start – but also how tenacious and creative you are in wanting to make them better.

For example, it might help to think about which of the four elements of trust need the most attention – competence, benevolence, integrity or predictability. And then, rather than making vague or blanket criticisms, to identify *specific* actions to address how a weakness in those elements affect *specific* aspects of your relationship/communication – from both sides. That is, by identifying your own contribution to creating whatever deadlock may currently exist, you can then take responsibility for getting from where you are now to where you want to be. There's no need to go public about this internal change; you just need to enact it, one creative conversation at a time (as Joel did when he decided to stop being so critical). Step-by-step, you could be amazed at the progress you make.

There's a power imbalance

Unequal power can be a huge obstacle to how we communicate with each other. Whether it's in a personal relationship, a family, an organisation small or large, or in wider society, who holds the power – or at least our perception of who holds the power – matters. It can determine who talks and who doesn't; who is heard and not heard; and what is and isn't on the table for discussion. If the power is exercised fairly most people will accept certain imbalances. They might say something like:

> *'Yes, maybe the seniors do always speak first, or are given the most time and attention, but they've earned that privilege because they've got the most experience and expertise – and anyway they always let others speak. They invite challenge and take those views into consideration.'*

But often power is not exercised fairly. It's used to restrict who can say what, when, where and how – and to whom. Or it's used to ignore what is inconvenient or threatening or simply deemed to be unimportant – because it matters only to those with less power (or none).

So what to do in situations like this? Can creative conversation make any real difference?

First, it has to be said that *any* relationship that denies basic human needs – whether it's on a personal, group or societal level – has to be challenged. Indeed, it's the refusal to accept relationships like this on a societal level that has driven – and continues to drive – great struggles for social justice. The civil rights movement in the USA, the feminist movement, the anti-apartheid movement in South Africa, the LGBT rights movement, the struggle for the rights of indigenous peoples in various parts of the world – all are (or have been) fuelled by the passion to correct a power imbalance that denies the needs for respect, equality and acceptance to particular groups of people. And it takes courage to challenge those who are misusing their power at any level, especially when they won't let it go without a fight – often literally.

More broadly, though, courage is the key to overcoming the obstacle of unequal power in *any* situation, even where the imbalance is simply that of a company hierarchy, say, or just the informal hierarchy of a family or social group. The kind of thinking that says *'I'm too junior to speak up'* or *'They're more important than me'* automatically puts up a barrier in our own mind to what's possible. And the attitude that says of some problem that *'It's too big, I'm too small and talking won't change anything anyway'* is the kind of thinking that tends to maintain the status quo, whether we like it or not.

So whatever the power balance in any relationship or situation, your first courageous act could be to challenge your own thinking. To put it another way, you can show courage by deciding, right now, to take responsibility for and be open-minded and creative in how you communicate in *all* your relationships.

Remember that the purpose of creative conversation is primarily to create or develop a connection with another person, maximising its bandwidth so that more and more understanding can flow back and forth along it. And that can be done to a lesser or greater extent with anybody. No one is stopping you from seeking to understand before seeking to be understood. You're free to challenge respectfully and positively, if you wish, and create deeper relationships rather than arguments. You can all do those things, anywhere, at any time, with *anyone*. Age, status and power dynamics are factors your Conversation Manager needs to take into account, yes – but only to find the best way to open up and then oversee the interaction.

In short, by deciding to practise creative conversation wherever there's a power imbalance you can effectively raise your 'status' by gaining a reputation for being a responsible, open-minded and creative presence at the centre of your own unique human network.

Wider change *might* come as result of this process – but it might not. There could be any number of reasons why what you want to see happen is not possible (or maybe even desirable). But by investing in creative conversation you will at least have a deeper understanding of the realities of the situation than you had at the outset, even if they're not to your liking. How you then act on that deeper understanding will be determined by your awareness of your own (possibly competing) needs and how you might meet them – for example, the need for security (so stay put) versus the need for expression (speak out) versus the need for justice (maybe join with others in the struggle) versus the need for freedom (maybe just walk away, if you can).

Bear in mind, too, that the bigger the challenge the more it moves beyond the purely personal. If you're trying to change organisational or societal culture you're also struggling on behalf of others and your actions will have a wider, possibly public, audience. But even here, so many of your interactions will be one-to-one or in small groups, and here again you'll reap the benefits of creative conversation – in gaining deeper understanding of people (including your opponents); in forging deeper connections; in preventing unnecessary escalation of conflicts; and, where possible, in reconciling after a struggle has been resolved. In fact, it could be that *you* are the only person in that situation demonstrating such a responsible, open-minded, creative approach – but your example might inspire someone else to behave similarly. Creative conversation really can be life-changing.

* * *

So far the discussion has assumed that you're in a position with little or no power. What, though, if you have a senior position, with seemingly *greater* power and authority, but are still in a situation that's stuck?

Here, once again, the way forward could be to challenge your own thinking, especially your perhaps unconscious attitude towards your power and authority. Might you secretly be guilty of thinking that '*I'm important and they're not*' when it comes to your juniors, or thinking that wisdom comes almost automatically with rank or status?

The reality is that *everyone's* view on situations in which they're involved contains something of value. Without embracing these different views it's impossible to develop a meaningful perspective. And, paradoxically, the greater the distance between any two people – through age or status, for example, or culture – the more meaningful the perspective that can potentially be gained through creative conversations between young and old, rich and poor, senior and junior, and different cultural groups.

Politicians who lose connection with their constituents; bosses who lose connection with their employees, suppliers and customers; head teachers who lose connection with their staff and students; and parents who lose connection with their children – all are in the same sinking boat. The person *at any level* who spots the leak, the thing that needs changing, has a choice – to take responsibility and speak up, or remain silent and let the boat wallow or even go down. But it's those who are senior who usually have the greater power to create the conditions in which everyone feels comfortable to say what needs to be said and then, where appropriate, to take the necessary action.

Wherever you are in a hierarchy or power structure, though – in fact, wherever you are *anywhere* – the challenge is to take the lament 'Why don't we talk?' and turn it into a positive invitation: 'Why don't we talk!'

And in that way, start your next – or very first – creative conversation.

Chapter 8

So What Now?

Let's return again to the question posed at the beginning of this book by Robert Waldinger, the fourth director of the Harvard Study of Adult Development.

'If you want to have a long, happy and fulfilled life, how should you invest your time and effort right now?'

The answer that came from the Harvard Study's 70-year analysis of the lives of more than 700 men was clear – 'Invest in your relationships.'

So how, this book has asked, can we do that? The answer, plainly and simply, lies in the way we communicate. Healthy relationships and healthy communication go hand-in-hand. And there's good reason for this. Just as we human beings are built to move, so we're built to communicate.

Millions of years of evolution have equipped us with the ability to see, hear, feel, describe, consider, comprehend, tell stories, question, argue and interpret; and then to reflect on our own thinking and re-evaluate it over time. When we talk to each other we combine our inner emotional lives with rational thought and natural instinct to exchange meaning, build relationships and get things done. These capacities have enabled us to grow in families, work in groups, live in communities and develop as societies and civilisations. Communication is as fundamental to our development as opposable thumbs and standing upright on two legs.

But if we don't use our legs much our muscles start to deteriorate, so when we do need to stand up and walk we don't get very far. The same 'use it or lose it' principle applies to engaging meaningfully with other people. Without regularly striving to understand others and be understood by them, our ability to 'get somewhere' in our relationships is compromised. Our lives feel smaller and the rich potential of the connections for which we're equipped goes undeveloped. So when we don't truly talk, don't truly listen, don't truly engage, we impoverish ourselves. This condition, which could be called 'communication deficiency', might not be as obvious to the eye as a physical disability but its effects are everywhere.

Levels of loneliness, isolation and polarisation in society continue to rise across the world. Despite having more channels through which to communicate than ever before, a 2018 survey[1] revealed that two-thirds of adults in the UK feel they have no one to talk to about their problems. Families, businesses, governments and international initiatives all suffer because poor personal communication stifles progress.

This is a human problem on a grand scale – and technology can't fix it. Only individual human beings – *you* – can fix it; and the principles and practices of creative conversation outlined in this book will definitely help.

That's because they've been distilled from the practical wisdom of many fields – counselling psychology, conflict management, nonviolent communication, negotiation skills – which focus on how we humans behave when we're at our best in sorting things out and making progress; how we build trust and resilience in our relationships, and how we create value.

Figure 8.1 is a visual summary of the basics of creative conversation. If you want to give it go it doesn't matter which principle or practice (or element of either) you start with. Creative conversations are inevitably unpredictable, so start

CREATIVE CONVERSATION

The
3 PRINCIPLES

RESPONSIBILITY	OPENNESS	CREATIVITY
for our conversations	to people	create connection
our relationships	to ideas	create trust
our networks	to challenge	create possibility

...and the
3 PRACTICES

UNDERSTANDING	CHALLENGING	BEING UNDERSTOOD
focus	tentative	tune in
stay open	invitational	set up
clarify	positive	paint the picture
summarise	specific	check

... address the
3 PAINS

PERSONAL	GROUPS	SOCIETAL
friends	teams	loneliness
relatives	businesses	fragmentation
neighbours	organisations	polarisation
colleagues		

... all of which are brought into play by your very own

CONVERSATION MANAGER

Figure 8.1 The basics of creative conversation

anywhere, with whichever principle, practice or element attracts you first. Responsibility, openness and creativity will always outdo negligence, closed-mindedness and negativity. Understanding, positive challenging and being understood will always win over confusion, bland acceptance and incoherence.

Wherever you start, though, you might like to think about setting out on your journey with some company. Research has shown that you're much more likely to embed new behaviour if you take action supported by – and supporting – at least two others, who also ideally know each other.[2] You can plan together, practise together, compare notes on your progress and encourage each other to keep trying to create 'something of value' in all the relationships that matter to you all. And a trio is *three* times stronger than just two people because a duo has only a single tie and so can be quite vulnerable. But with two companions there are three ties. Add one more for a quartet and the number of ties *doubles* to six.[3] So there's strength even in small numbers.

But whether you decide to become a talking revolutionary alone or in a pair or with a cadre of comrades, choose the right entry-point for you, start with your very next conversation – and see what happens. And when something does, let us know at **www.thetalkingrevolution.org**, where you'll also find more resources to help you.

We need a revolution. So let's talk. Oh – and spread the word!

Notes

Introduction

1 *The Forgotten Role of Families* (Centre for Social Justice, 2017).
2 American Psychological Association (5 August 2017). 'Social isolation, loneliness could be greater threat to public health than obesity', *Science Daily*.
3 'Trapped in a bubble: an investigation into triggers for loneliness in the UK', Co-op/British Red Cross (December 2016).
4 American systems scientist (b. 1947) and author of *The Fifth Discipline: The Art and Practice of the Learning Organization* (1990; rev. 2006).
5 From the Foreword to *Dialogue and the Art of Thinking Together* by William Isaacs (1999).
6 Michael Kruse, 'The wall that Trump actually built', *Politico Magazine* (Jan/Feb 2018).
7 Kruse first visited Pepin County at the end of 2016 and wrote this article after his second visit a year later.
8 Japanese Buddhist writer and thinker (b. 1928).

Chapter 1

1 https://www.ted.com/talks/robert_waldinger_what_makes_a_good_life_lessons_from_the_longest_study_on_happiness?c=313016&utm_campaign=tedspread&utm_medium=referral&utm_source=tedcomshare
2 Andrew Clark, Sarah Fleche, Richard Layard, Nattavudh Powdthavee, and George Ward, 'Origins of happiness: evidence and policy implications', LSE (December 2016).
3 Ben Wedeman, 'How to live to 100: town full of centenarians spills its secrets', CNN (October 2016).
4 American author and family counsellor (1940–2016).
5 See, for example, The Bucharest Early Intervention Project, a collaboration between Tulane University, the University of Maryland and Boston Children's Hospital, http://www.bucharestearlyinterventionproject.org/index.html.
6 Private interview, 2008.
7 See for example, Julianne Holt-Lunstad et al., 'Loneliness and social isolation as risk factors for mortality: a meta-analytic review', Department of Psychology and Department of Counseling Psychology, Brigham Young University.

8   American author and rabbi (1929–2002).
9   Both figures as of 2018.

Chapter 2

1   Or use this formula to work it out: $n \times (n - 1) \div 2$, where n is the total number of people. In our examples, $10 \times 9 \div 2 = 45$ and $20 \times 19 \div 2 = 190$.
2   D. Centola et al., 'Experimental evidence for tipping points in social convention', *Science* (2018).
3   For example, see the work of Professor Miles Hewstone at the Oxford Centre for the Study of Intergroup Conflict – https://www.psy.ox.ac.uk/research/the-oxford-centre-for-the-study-of-intergroup-conflict-oxcsic. See also Katherine W. Phillips, 'How diversity makes us smarter', *Scientific American* (October 2014); and Debra Umberson and Jennifer Karas Montez, 'Social relationships and health: a flashpoint for health policy', *Journal of Health and Social Behavior* (October 2010).
4   Japanese Buddhist priest (1222–1283).
5   American author and organisational expert (1932–2012).
6   *The 7 Habits of Highly Effective People* (1988).
7   See, for example, Scott Atran's *Talking to the Enemy: Sacred Values, Violent Extremism, and What it Means to be Human* (2011).
8   *The Influential Mind: What the Brain Reveals About Our Power to Change Others* (2017).
9   See Jonas T. Kaplan, Sarah I. Gimbel and Sam Harris, 'Neural correlates of maintaining one's political beliefs in the face of counter-evidence', *Scientific Reports*, Vol. 6 (2016).
10 'Moral outrage in the digital age', *Nature Human Behaviour* (September 2017).
11 Roman playwright (185–159 BC).
12 American psychologist and author (1934–2015).
13 *Nonviolent Communication: A Language of Life* (2003).
14 William Isaacs, *Dialogue and the Art of Thinking Together* (1999).
15 Karen Littleton and Neil Mercer, *Interthinking: Putting Talk to Work* (2014).
16 *Letter Report LR ST1405AL00*, DRDC, Toronto Research Centre (2013).

Part Two

1   Gerard Egan, *The Skilled Helper: A Problem Management and Opportunity Development Approach to Helping* (1975; 11th edition, 2018).
2   Abby Rockefeller Mauzé Professor of the Social Studies of Science and Technology at the Massachusetts Institute of Technology.

3 Sherry Turkle, *Reclaiming Conversation: The Power of Talk in a Digital Age* (2015).

Chapter 3
1 American author (b. 1934).
2 Dutch philosopher (1632–77).

Chapter 4
1 Along with another 'serving-man' Kipling doesn't mention – **Whether** (to challenge). This question is explored in Chapter 7 – Why Don't We Talk?
2 Bangladeshi economist and Nobel Peace Prize Laureate (b. 1940).
3 American musician (b. 1947).
4 Marshall Rosenberg, *Nonviolent Communication: A Language of Life* (2003).

Chapter 5
1 French playwright (1622–73).
2 George Canning, British statesman and politician (1770–1827).
3 French playwright (1910–87).
4 Heraclitus of Ephesus (c. 535–475 BCE); quoted by Socrates in Plato's *Cratylus*, 402a.

Chapter 6
1 American poet (1803–82).
2 English writer and lexicographer (1709–84).
3 Posited by the American attorney and author Mike Godwin in 1990, originally in relation to Usenet newsgroup discussions.

Chapter 7
1 English physicist and cosmologist (1942–2018).
2 'Enforcing dialogue' can work the other way too; that is, at times you might have to strongly encourage the other person to speak and use the full range of your understander skills to draw them out. See 'Prompts and probes', pp. 89–91.

Chapter 8
1 Time for Change, February 2018, https://www.time-to-change.org.uk/news/two-thirds-people-feel-they-have-no-one-talk-about-personal-problems-such-mental-health.
2 Damon Centola, *How Behavior Spreads: The Science of Complex Contagions*, 2018.
3 $4 \times 3 \div 2 = 6$. See Chapter 2, footnote 1 above.

Some Basic Human Needs – Which Are Most Important to You?

PHYSICAL

- *air*
- *food*
- *health*
- *movement*
- *safety*
- *sex*
- *shelter*
- *sleep*
- *touch*
- *warmth*
- *water*

EMOTIONAL/PSYCHOLOGICAL

- *acceptance*
- *accuracy*
- *achievement*
- *acknowledgment*
- *appreciation*
- *authenticity*
- *beauty*
- *challenge*
- *choice*
- *clarity*
- *coherence*
- *communication*
- *community*
- *company*
- *compassion*
- *connection*
- *consideration*
- *consistency*
- *continuity*
- *control*
- *creativity*
- *economy*
- *effectiveness*
- *empathy*
- *fairness*
- *freedom*
- *friendship*
- *fulfilment*
- *growth*
- *harmony*
- *to help*
- *honesty*
- *hope*
- *humour*
- *influence*
- *inspiration*
- *integrity*
- *joy*
- *learning*

- *logic*
- *love*
- *meaning*
- *nature*
- *novelty*
- *order*
- *peace*
- *play (fun)*
- *positive (self) regard*
- *power*
- *privacy*
- *quality*
- *relevance*
- *reliability*
- *respect*
- *resolution*
- *self-expression*
- *sincerity*
- *spirituality*
- *stability*
- *status*
- *stimulation*
- *support*
- *to nurture*
- *trust*
- *understanding*

'I LOVE IT WHEN…', 'I HATE IT WHEN…'

To get some idea of which needs are most important to you and so inform your values, here's a simple exercise.

Write five sentences that begin with the words 'I love it when…'. These are people, things and situations you really treasure and enjoy.

Then write five sentences that begin with the words 'I hate it when…'. These are people, things and situations you really dislike and don't enjoy.

Now, we tend to be positive about people, things and situations that meet our needs and negative about people, things and situations when they fail to meet our needs or actively block them.

So take each sentence and circle which of your needs might be relevant to that love or hate. There might be several at play in each case.

For example, if you say 'I love it when the sun shines' that might be because that meets your needs for *warmth, movement, nature* and *hope* – various needs that you subjectively associate with the sun shining.

On the other hand, if you say 'I hate it when it's cold and rainy' you might be also expressing your needs for *warmth, movement, nature* and *hope,* only this time through their absence.

After working through all ten sentences in this way have a look at the needs you've circled. Is there a pattern? Do they confirm your idea of yourself – or surprise you? Are these the basis of your values? And how might what you see here be relevant to other aspects of your life and relationships?

APPENDIX B

Thinking Outside the Box

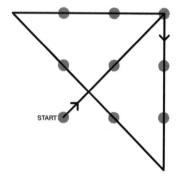

START

Answer: You have to think outside the box.

APPENDIX C

Our Personal Journeys

Here's a little more about ourselves and why, by different routes, we've reached a point where we believe a talking revolution is not just essential but possible. *Doable*. Right now.

The roots of Peter's passion for this subject reach right back to his family upbringing in West London.

I never had a proper conversation with my father. He was a generous, responsible, caring man, and we could always talk about sport or the weather or how to get from A to B, but whenever anything difficult came up – like my grandmother dying or why my mum never left the house (I later found out she was agoraphobic) – the answer would be 'You don't want to know about that.'

The trouble was, I did want to know about it.

Curiously, the more important a subject was, the more likely it was to be swept under the family carpet. The older I got, the more the frustrated I became with the culture of silence, especially around my mum's condition. Mental illness in 1950s London, although very common in the wake of the Second World War, was a shameful subject. On top of that, my parents, while coping as best they could with the illness and the stigma, had no experience from their own upbringing of sitting down and talking things through. So my mum and dad, my sister and I were stranded in a kind of conversational desert, which none of us consciously chose or liked.

It would have been good to talk, as they say, but we didn't know how. Not talking was just how things were. Fears and feelings went unexpressed, stories went untold and questions, if asked at all, went unanswered. Boy, was it dull, not to mention deeply frustrating. I don't know, even now, quite what I wanted to talk to my dad about, but looking back I can certainly recognise in my teenage self a need for a level of connection with my parents which, for all their great qualities, we never seemed able to achieve.

So I left home, aged sixteen, and almost immediately made a remarkable discovery. Rick and Min lived with their two young daughters a few doors down from my new place. It was the year when TV went from black-and-white to colour, and the difference between my family culture and theirs was just as revolutionary.

They told each other things.

They wanted to know what was happening in each other's lives.

They had rows, and laughed, and fell out and made up.

They had their challenges as a family too, of course, but at least things were expressed – often very colourfully. Until I met them, I honestly didn't know that families could be like that. I'd certainly never met one. For all its craziness, there was also something deeply sane about Rick and Min's house. And I remember thinking, 'When I have a home and a family, I want it to be like this.'

That happened. Gayle and I had two children, a boy and girl. We talked a lot together, and listened to what they had to say. While they were growing up, I got the chance to work on a UK-wide project to promote the skills of dialogue in schools. It was perfect for me. I jumped at it – and almost immediately two things became very clear. First, this not-communicating thing wasn't limited to just my childhood, my family and the people we knew. There were problems all over – in families, schools, businesses, government, everywhere. But, second, something practical could be done about it.

Years later, when Gayle was dying of cancer and life was at its hardest, I saw how our family culture of always talking with our son and daughter had helped them; not just to cope with their mum's illness and death, but to develop into open-minded, wise, well-balanced young adults, comfortable with people and able to deal with life's challenges in a way that my own upbringing certainly hadn't prepared me.

It's conversation that makes the difference – creative *conversation. That's clear to me now, and my purpose in writing this book is to encourage everyone to do more of it.*

Eddy's interest in creative conversation is closely bound up with a deep desire to understand conflict and how it can be resolved or managed without violence.

I was part of a post-war generation of young boys that grew up on a diet of comics like The Hotspur *and* The Victor *that celebrated the heroics of the British military in the fight against fascism. And as a young schoolboy I spent hours and hours playing war games with a like-minded friend, refighting the fall of France, the North Africa campaign and the invasion of Italy.*

But in my early teens everything changed. I learnt about the First World War and read the poems of Wilfred Owen and my enthusiasm for all things military disappeared. Many people go through an anti-war phase in their adolescence but 'grow out of it' as they get older. I didn't. In fact, after the Falklands War in 1982 I joined an organisation that promoted nonviolence and dialogue as an alternative to war, and for many years supported its activities.

Then on 11 September 2001 things changed for me again as, in real time on a large flat screen TV, I watched the Twin Towers come crashing down. Like most of the world I was shocked and confused. Why had this happened? Who were Al Qaeda? And why were they so monstrously, murderously angry? I didn't have a clue and didn't know who I could ask. To my shame, I realised that I didn't even know any Muslims. A period of honest reflection threw up the uncomfortable conclusion that I'd been living in a kind of a bubble, a comfortable cocoon. And that if I really wanted to help make a difference I had to connect more directly with the world.

So began for me a journey of exploration into the dynamics of conflict – at all levels and of all kinds – and into whether and how talking really can act as the most effective insurance policy against conflict turning violent.

It started with a visit to my local mosque, which led me to my local interfaith group, which led to encounters with local, then national politicians and meetings in Parliament; which, following the invasion of Iraq, led to me helping set up and then run for ten years an All-Party Parliamentary Group focused on how to prevent, resolve and transform violent conflict. My journey has taken me to North and South America, Africa, the Middle East, the Caucasus and all round Europe; and, ironically, it eventually saw me for almost four years co-leading with two British Army officers an international project on how, practically, military actors can best contribute to the prevention of violent conflict.

It also led me to Peter Osborn. I'd known Peter since the late 1980s – we were both volunteers in the peace organisation I joined after the Falklands War – but I'd never really understood what he actually did. Until one day a long, creative conversation revealed that our areas of work had an enormous amount of overlap. We've been collaborating on and off ever since on how to make talking more effective, both in helping people to connect with each other and in resolving conflict. And at regular intervals, we've told each other that 'One day, we really must write all this down.'

So now, finally, we have.

37575866R00130

Made in the USA
Middletown, DE
28 February 2019